E·A·S·Y
FRENCH
EXERCISES

Practice
for Beginners

Stephanie Rybak
Series Editor, Brian Hill

Printed on recyclable paper

PASSPORT BOOKS
a division of *NTC Publishing Group*
Lincolnwood, Illinois USA

Acknowledgments

The author and publishers wish to thank the following for permission
to use material: La Régie Autonome des Transports Parisiens for
reproduction of the Paris métro map, 58 B 6348, RATP on page 29;
J. Allan Cash Ltd. for the photographs on pages 39 and 53;
Gîtes de France for the use of their logo on page 74.

Every effort has been made to trace all the copyright holders, but if
any have been inadvertently overlooked, the publishers will be pleased
to make the necessary arrangement at the first opportunity.

This edition first published 1996 by Passport Books, a division of NTC Publishing Group,
4255 West Touhy Avenue, Lincolnwood (Chicago), Illinois 60646-1975 U.S.A.

First published 1994 by
THE MACMILLAN PRESS LTD.
Houndmills, Basingstoke, Hampshire RG21 2XS
and London

Manufactured in the United States of America.

6 7 8 9 ML 0 9 8 7 6 5 4 3 2 1

Contents

Introduction

Easy French Exercises is a new self-study resource for language learners. First and foremost it is designed to provide extra practice in reading and writing skills in a digestible, enjoyable, and easy-to-follow format.

The book is related to the content of the successful *Just Listen 'n Learn French* course and will certainly be welcomed by learners who are using or have used *Just Listen 'n Learn*, but it is of equal value to people who have had other exposure to the language. The book takes as its starting point the crucial topics you need when visiting or developing contacts abroad. So you find yourself involved in activities to help you when you are introducing yourself; describing your family, your job, or your town; asking for directions; shopping; ordering meals or making reservations; saying what you like or dislike; talking about your vacation; or saying good-bye.

The book is particularly appropriate for people who have made reasonable progress in listening and speaking, but who feel they now need something a bit more concrete to reinforce the vocabulary and structures they have learned. The activities, therefore, have been carefully selected to practice key language points in an enjoyable way.

Everything is carefully explained, and you should have no difficulty knowing what you are expected to do. At the end of each unit are full answers, so you can check how you are doing. These have been made as comprehensive as possible, so you can figure out where you went wrong.

Everybody works at a different pace, but on the average you should expect to spend from 1 to 1½ hours working through each unit. It is a good idea to have a dictionary handy to check on any words you don't know.

You might also find it fun to work on the book with somebody else in your family or with friends. Two or three heads are better than one, and you can help each other. You can work at home, on your lunch breaks, or even on the plane or train.

Easy French Exercises is ideal for practicing, reviewing, and developing your language skills in an easy way that nevertheless covers the ground thoroughly. When you feel that you have mastered the activities in the 15 units, you will have a sound base to make the most of your vacation, visits from friends, and the many situations where language skills open up formerly closed doors.

Brian Hill
Series Editor

1   TALKING ABOUT YOURSELF

Exercise 1   Let's start by reviewing a few basic words and phrases. See if you can write the number of the correct translation (1–10) by each French item.

a.	**Bonsoir!**	....	1	I am on vacation.
b.	**Bonne nuit!**	....	2	Good night!
c.	**Vous êtes de Paris?**	....	3	I live in Paris.
d.	**J'habite Paris.**	....	4	(Have a) good vacation!
e.	**Vous êtes français?**	....	5	Are you French?
f.	**Je suis français.**	....	6	Are you American?
g.	**Je suis américain.**	....	7	Good evening!
h.	**Vous êtes américain?**	....	8	I am French.
i.	**Je suis en vacances.**	....	9	I am American.
j.	**Bonnes vacances!**	....	10	Are you from Paris?

The answers to all the exercises are at the end of the unit.

Exercise 2   Circle the word that doesn't belong in each of these sets of words.

a. **Mademoiselle / Messieurs-dames / Merci / Monsieur**

b. **Bonjour / C'est / Au revoir / Bonsoir**

c. **Nom / Adresse / Prénom / Bière**

d. **Américain / Londres / Anglais / Australien**

e. **Vous / Il / Nous / Quoi**

Exercise 3   Here is part of a hotel's market-research questionnaire:

Nom: (Monsieur/Madame/Mademoiselle) ....

Prénom: ....

Adresse: ....

....

Nationalité: ....

Je suis...   avec un groupe   ☐

avec ma famille   ☐

tout seul / toute seule   ☐

Fill it in / delete as appropriate as though you were Mrs. Barbara Carter, an American woman traveling with a group. Her home address is 34 Parker Street, Buffalo, New York.

Exercise 4   You can probably guess the meanings of these words for nationalities. Which of the speakers (a–g) are women?

a. **Je suis anglais.**   ☐

b. **Je suis française.**   ☐

c. **Je suis américain.**   ☐

d. **Je suis hollandaise.**   ☐

e. **Je suis italien.**   ☐

f. **Je suis portugaise.**   ☐

g. **Je suis grec.**   ☐

Exercise 5   Now write the nationalities of these people:

a.   Il est de Washington.   Il est   ....

b.   Il est d'Athènes.   Il est   ....

c.   Il est de Rome.   Il est   ....

d.   Elle est d'Amsterdam.   Elle est   ....

e.   Elle est de Lisbonne.   Elle est   ....

f.   Il est de Londres.   Il est   ....

g.   Elle est de Paris.   Elle est   ....

Exercise 6   Read what these four people tell you about themselves and then see if you can answer the questions below.

1   Bonjour! Je suis français – j'habite Paris. Je suis en vacances à Londres avec ma famille.

2   Bonjour! Je suis française. J'habite toute seule à Londres.

3   Bonjour! Je suis américaine. Je suis de Washington. Je suis touriste – je suis en vacances à Paris avec un groupe.

4   Bonjour! Je suis américain. J'habite Paris – avec ma famille.

Of the four speakers,

		1	2	3	4
a.	Who are women?	☐	☐	☐	☐
b.	Who lives in London?	☐	☐	☐	☐
c.	Who is American?	☐	☐	☐	☐
d.	Who live in Paris?	☐	☐	☐	☐
e.	Who says he/she lives alone?	☐	☐	☐	☐
f.	Who is on vacation?	☐	☐	☐	☐

Exercise 7 Two people meet in the bar at a conference. The lines of their conversation are given in the wrong order. Can you write them out correctly?

Monsieur Meadows	Je suis de New York.
Madame Tessier	Je suis française.
Monsieur Meadows	Bonsoir, Madame.
Madame Tessier	Vous êtes français?
Monsieur Meadows	Vous habitez Paris?
Madame Tessier	Bonsoir, Monsieur.
Monsieur Meadows	Non, je suis américain. Et vous?
Madame Tessier	Non, j'habite Nantes. Et vous?

Madame Tessier	....
Monsieur Meadows	....
Madame Tessier	....
Monsieur Meadows	....
Madame Tessier	....
Monsieur Meadows	....
Madame Tessier	....
Monsieur Meadows	....

Exercise 8 Hidden in the word square are the French words for:

please	thank you	good evening	good bye
yes	no	'Sir'	family	vacation	beer

French (in the masculine)   English (in the feminine)

live (as in 'I live')   you   London

five of the numbers between three and ten

The French words are written across (left to right) or down, with some letters used in more than one word. Can you find and circle all the words? (Accents are not usually used in word squares and crosswords.)

S	F	A	M	I	L	L	E	O	P	O	H
I	R	V	O	U	S	T	Z	U	T	T	A
L	A	A	U	R	E	V	O	I	R	R	B
V	N	L	M	S	N	E	U	F	U	O	I
O	Ç	V	N	O	N	M	E	R	C	I	T
U	A	Q	U	A	T	R	E	R	T	S	E
S	I	A	N	G	L	A	I	S	E	F	G
P	S	E	P	T	H	U	I	T	S	F	X
L	O	N	D	R	E	S	B	I	E	R	E
A	T	O	E	M	O	N	S	I	E	U	R
I	Q	F	L	M	B	O	N	S	O	I	R
T	A	A	V	A	C	A	N	C	E	S	B

ANSWERS

Exercise 1
a. 7 **b.** 2 **c.** 10 **d.** 3 **e.** 5 **f.** 8 **g.** 9 **h.** 6 **i.** 1 **j.** 4

Exercise 2
a. Merci **b.** C'est **c.** Bière **d.** Londres **e.** Quoi

Exercise 3
Nom: Madame Carter; Prénom: Barbara; Nationalité: Américaine;
Je suis... avec un groupe

Exercise 4
b, **d** and **f** are women, because the adjectives are in the feminine
(with an **-e** on the end). The masculine forms would be **français**,
hollandais and **portugais**.

Exercise 5
a. Il est américain. (Check that you remembered the accent – and that it
was sloping in the right direction.) **b.** Il est grec. **c.** Il est italien.
d. Elle est hollandaise. (Remember that feminine adjectives end in
an **-e**.) **e.** Elle est portugaise. **f.** Il est anglais. **g.** Elle est française.
(Don't forget the cedilla under the **c**.)

Exercise 6
a. 2, 3 **b.** 2 **c.** 3, 4 **d.** 1, 4 **e.** 2 **f.** 1, 3

Exercise 7
Madame Tessier	Bonsoir, Monsieur.
Monsieur Meadows	Bonsoir, Madame.
Madame Tessier	Vous êtes français?
Monsieur Meadows	Non, je suis américain. Et vous?
Madame Tessier	Je suis française.
Monsieur Meadows	Vous habitez Paris?
Madame Tessier	Non, j'habite Nantes. Et vous?
Monsieur Meadows	Je suis de New York.

Exercise 8
The hidden words are:
s'il vous plaît, merci,
bonsoir, au revoir, oui,
non, monsieur, famille,
vacances, bière, français,
anglaise, habite, vous,
Londres, trois, quatre, sept,
huit, neuf

S	F	A	M	I	L	L	E	O	P	O	H
I	R	V	O	U	S	T	Z	U	T	T	A
L	A	A	U	R	E	V	O	I	R	R	B
V	N	L	M	S	N	E	U	F	U	O	I
O	ç	V	N	O	N	M	E	R	C	I	T
U	A	Q	U	A	T	R	E	R	T	S	E
S	I	A	N	G	L	A	I	S	E	F	G
P	S	E	P	T	H	U	I	T	S	F	X
L	O	N	D	R	E	S	B	I	E	R	E
A	T	O	E	M	O	N	S	I	E	U	R
I	Q	F	L	M	B	O	N	S	O	I	R
T	A	A	V	A	C	A	N	C	E	S	B

Je suis dentiste

Exercise 1 *Jobsearch*

If you fill in the names of the jobs across, the shaded vertical column will show another.

a. hairdresser

b. accountant

c. secretary

d. civil servant

e. plumber

f. engineer

g. store owner

The answers to all the exercises are at the end of the unit.

Exercise 2   Here are some more occupations. Write **Il est ...** or **Elle est ...** and the appropriate job by each of the pictures.

réceptionniste	dentiste	médecin
professeur	homme d'affaires	

a. ....   b. ....   c. ....

....

d. ....   e. ....

....

Exercise 3   Who is the single mother (**la mère célibataire**) out of these four sisters?

Claire est la sœur de Julie, de Céline et de Jeanne-Marie.

Claire a deux enfants.

Julie a trois enfants.

Céline n'a pas d'enfants.

Jeanne-Marie a une fille.

Claire et Julie sont mariées.

Céline et Jeanne-Marie ne sont pas mariées.

Exercise 4   What language do these people have in common? Are any of the
languages mentioned spoken by none of them?

New words: **allemand** (German) and **espagnol** (Spanish)

Joanna parle anglais.
Elle parle espagnol.
Elle parle allemand.
Elle ne parle pas français.
Elle ne parle pas italien.
Elle ne parle pas portugais.

Franz parle allemand.
Il parle anglais.
Il parle français.
Il parle espagnol.
Il ne parle pas italien.
Il ne parle pas portugais.

Enrico parle espagnol.
Il parle portugais.
Il ne parle pas anglais.
Il ne parle pas français.
Il ne parle pas allemand.
Il ne parle pas italien.

Sophie parle français.
Elle parle anglais.
Elle parle italien.
Elle parle espagnol.
Elle ne parle pas allemand.
Elle ne parle pas portugais.

See if you can fill in the missing vowels in these negative statements. There are clues on the next page, but you might like to see if you can fill in some of the missing letters even before you look at the clues.

New word: **la paix** (peace)

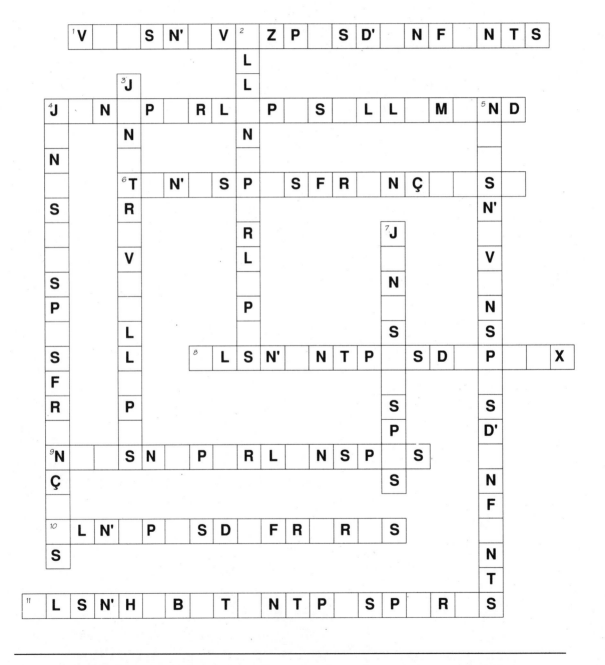

Across

1   You don't have any children
4   I don't speak German
6   You (a close female friend) are not French
8   They have no peace
9   We are not speaking
10 He doesn't have any brothers
11 They don't live in Paris

Down

2   She is not speaking
3   I don't work
4   I (masculine) am not French
5   We don't have any children
7   I don't know

Exercise 6   You have received a particularly annoying letter from a French company claiming (wrongly) to know all about you. Since they have sent a postage-paid return envelope, you take the trouble to write out a contradiction after each of the claims they make about you (**Non, je ne suis pas français**, etc.).

---

a.   **Vous êtes français.**

....

b.   **Vous habitez Versailles.**

....

c.   **Vous êtes homme d'affaires.**

....

d.   **Vous travaillez dans un bureau à Paris.**

....

e.   **Vous êtes marié depuis vingt ans.**

....

f.   **Vous avez deux enfants.**

....

g.   **Vous parlez allemand.**

....

ANSWERS

Exercise 1

a. coiffeur **b.** comptable **c.** secrétaire **d.** fonctionnaire
e. plombier **f.** ingénieur **g.** commerçant; **Vertical word:** facteur

Exercise 2

a. Il est homme d'affaires. **b.** Il est médecin. **c.** Elle est dentiste.
d. Elle est professeur. **e.** Elle est réceptionniste.

Exercise 3

Jeanne-Marie

Exercise 4

Spanish; No

Exercise 5

Across:
1. VOUS N'AVEZ PAS D'ENFANTS
4. JE NE PARLE PAS ALLEMAND
6. TU N'ES PAS FRANÇAISE
8. ILS N'ONT PAS DE PAIX
9. NOUS NE PARLONS PAS
10. IL N'A PAS DE FRERES
11. ILS N'HABITENT PAS PARIS

Down:
2. ELLE NE PARLE PAS
3. JE NE TRAVAILLE PAS
   JE NE SUIS PAS FRANÇAIS
5. NOUS N'AVONS PAS D'ENFANTS
7. JE NE SAIS PAS

Exercise 6

a. Non, je ne suis pas français. **b.** Non, je n'habite pas Versailles.
c. Non, je ne suis pas homme d'affaires. **d.** Non, je ne travaille pas
dans un bureau à Paris. **e.** Non, je ne suis pas marié depuis vingt
ans. **f.** Non, je n'ai pas deux enfants. (OR Non, je n'ai pas d'enfants.)
g. Non, je ne parle pas allemand.

And you may have wished to add: **Je suis une femme!**

ORDERING DRINKS AND SNACKS

Exercise 1 Can you complete this card to order breakfast in your hotel room? You and your family want:

- four full continental breakfasts with
- one coffee with milk
- one tea
- one hot chocolate
- one cold milk
- four orange juices
- four eggs

Hôtel de la Paix

	Nombre	*En supplément*	*Nombre*
Petit déjeuner complet	☐	Jus de tomate	☐
		Jus d'orange	☐
Café			
– noir	☐	Jambon	☐
– au lait	☐	Oeuf	☐
		Fromage	☐
Thé			
– nature	☐		
– au citron	☐		
– au lait	☐		
Chocolat			
– chaud	☐		
– froid	☐		
Lait			
– chaud	☐		
– froid	☐		

The answers to all the exercises are at the end of the unit.

Exercise 2 Can you unscramble this breakfast order for five people?

- **a.** QINC TIPETS JEREDUNES POMLECTS
- **b.** CAVE...
- **c.** NU FACE UA ALTI
- **d.** NU CEAF RONI
- **e.** NU HET AU CRITNO
- **f.** NU TEH VACE UD ALIT DROFI
- **g.** NU TALI DUCHA

Exercise 3

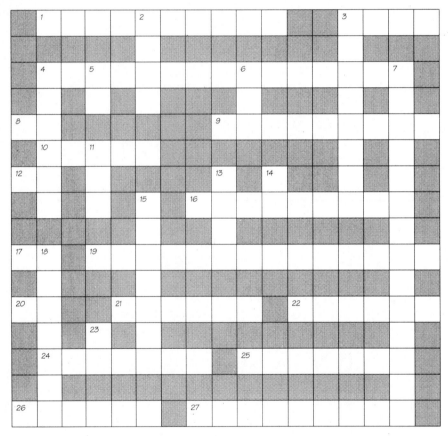

Reviewing the following words and phrases will help you with the crossword, even though they are not exactly the same as any of the answers:

à boire   to drink / for drinking
la galette au jambon   pancake with ham
le sandwich aux rillettes   cold cut sandwich
le croque-madame   toasted ham and cheese sandwich with
                                           an egg on top
le sorbet au citron   lemon sherbet

Across

1	What'll you have? **Qu'est-ce que** ....? (4, 6)
3	Seven (4)
4	Pancake with eggs (7, 3, 5)
8	Is it **le** or **la bouteille**? (2)
9	Some beer (2, 2, 5)
10	Cider (5)
12	Is it **le** or **la sandwich**? (2)
16	A soft French cheese (9)
17	Is it **le** or **la pression**? (2)
19	Toasted ham and cheese sandwich (6, 8)
20	Is it **le** or **la vodka**? (2)
21	Ham (6)
22	Baked circles of dough with cheese, etc., on top (6)
24	Cheese named after a Swiss region (7)
25	Frankfurters on buns (3, 4)
26	I'll have: **Je** .... (6)
27	Cold cuts (9)

Down

2	Liver/chicken pâté (4)
3	Sausage (8)
4	Ice cream (6)
5	Is it **le** or **la petit déjeuner**? (2)
6	Feminine of **un** (3)
7	Black currant sherbet(6, 2, 6)
11	Some (plural) (3)
13	Drink or drinking place (4)
14	Is it **le** or **la citron**? (2)
15	Cheese (7)
18	To eat / for eating (1, 6)
23	Some (masculine singular) (2)

Exercise 4   The figures in French telephone numbers are said in pairs. For example, the number 13.15.11.02 would be said: **Treize. Quinze. Onze. Zéro Deux.** Write out how you would say the following telephone numbers in French:

a.   20.16.18.07   ....

b.   15.13.12.19   ....

c.   12.15.17.08   ....

d.   18.05.16.15   ....

e.   11.13.04.14   ....

f.   12.14.16.20   ....

Exercise 5   Fill in the blanks in the conversation using the following phrases. You will need to use one of them twice.

qu'est-ce que	qu'est-ce que vous voulez
qu'est-ce que vous avez	qu'est-ce que vous avez comme

Garçon de café   Bonjour, Madame. .... vous prenez?

Madame Latour   Bonjour, Monsieur. .... à manger, s'il vous plaît?

Garçon de café   A manger? Nous avons des pizzas, des croque-monsieur et des sandwichs.

Madame Latour   .... sandwichs?

Garçon de café   Comme sandwichs: jambon, fromage, pâté, rillettes.

Madame Latour   Un sandwich au jambon, s'il vous plaît.

Garçon de café   Très bien. Et .... boire, Madame?

Madame Latour   .... bière?

Garçon de café   Comme bière nous avons de la pression – c'est une bière allemande – et de la Kronenbourg en bouteilles.

Madame Latour   Une pression, s'il vous plaît.

Garçon de café   Parfait.

Exercise 6   Here are two brief exchanges which you have with your hostess, Madame Trognon. In the first one, all the missing words are parts of the verb **prendre**. In the second, they are **du**, **de la** and **des**. Can you fill in the blanks correctly? You may not know the word for 'bread': **le pain**.

First exchange

Madame Trognon   Qu'est-ce que vous .... pour le petit déjeuner?

Vous   Patrick .... du café noir. Les enfants ....

du chocolat chaud. Et moi, je .... un thé avec du

lait froid, s'il vous plaît.

Second exchange

Madame Trognon   Alors, qu'est-ce que vous avez pour le pique-nique?

Vous   .... jambon, ... fromage,

.... pain, ... bière, ... Coca,

.... oranges et .... chocolat.

ANSWERS

Exercise 1

Petit déjeuner complet 4; Café au lait 1; Thé au lait 1; Chocolat chaud 1; Lait froid 1; Jus d'orange 4; Oeuf 4

Exercise 2

a. cinq petits déjeuners complets **b.** avec... **c.** un café au lait
d. un café noir **e.** un thé au citron **f.** un thé avec du lait froid
g. un lait chaud

Exercise 3

```
V O U S P R E N E Z     S E P T
      A                 A
  G A L E T T E A U X O E U F S
  L   E   E         N     C   O
L A           D E L A B I E R E
  C I D R E             S   B
L E   E         C   L   S   E
  S   S   F   C A M E M B E R T
          R   F             A
L A   C R O Q U E M O N S I E U R
  M       M                 C
L A     J A M B O N   P I Z Z A S
  N   D G                   S
  G R U Y E R E   H O T D O G S
  E                         I
P R E N D S   R I L L E T T E S
```

Exercise 4

a. Vingt. Seize. Dix-huit. Zéro Sept **b.** Quinze. Treize. Douze. Dix-neuf **c.** Douze. Quinze. Dix-sept. Zéro Huit **d.** Dix-huit. Zéro Cinq. Seize. Quinze **e.** Onze. Treize. Zéro Quatre. Quatorze **f.** Douze. Quatorze. Seize. Vingt

Exercise 5

qu'est-ce que; qu'est-ce que vous avez; qu'est-ce que vous avez comme; qu'est-ce que vous voulez; qu'est-ce que vous avez comme

Exercise 6

First exchange

Madame Trognon Qu'est-ce que vous prenez pour le petit déjeuner?
Vous Patrick prend du café noir. Les enfants prennent du chocolat chaud. Et moi, je prends un thé avec du lait froid, s'il vous plaît.

Second exchange

Madame Trognon Alors, qu'est-ce que vous avez pour le pique-nique?
Vous Du jambon, du fromage, du pain, de la bière, du Coca, des oranges et du chocolat.

Exercise 1 *Fishing for information*

Which reply is each of the questions fishing for?

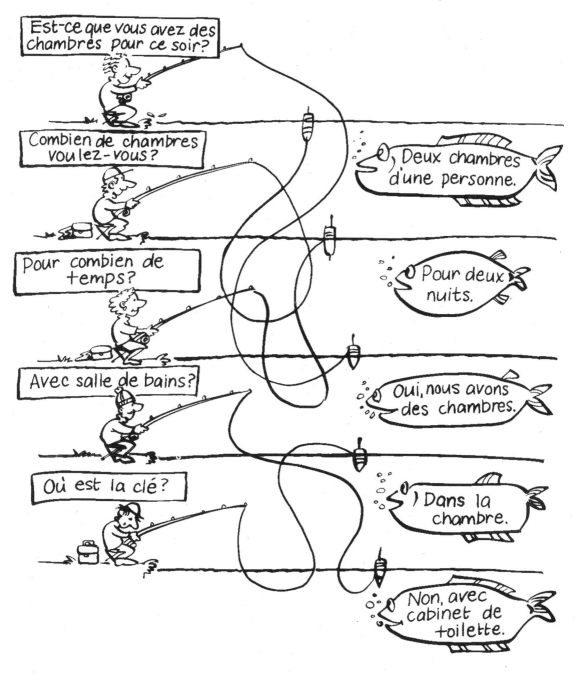

Exercise 2 In these sentences, all the words beginning with the letter **c** have been removed and put in the box below. Can you put them back in the correct blanks?

a. Où peut-on .... des .... de voyage, s'il vous plaît?

b. Vous voulez une .... avec douche ou avec .... de toilette?

c. Je ne .... pas – je suis anglais.

d. Vous pouvez me .... par lettre?

e. .... de jours vous voulez rester?

confirmer	cabinet	chèques	combien
changer	comprends	chambre	

Exercise 3 Read this conversation between a customer and a hotel receptionist and then see if you can write in French the answers to the questions that follow.

Client	Bonjour, Monsieur.
Réceptionniste	Bonjour, Monsieur.
Client	Vous avez des chambres pour ce soir, s'il vous plaît?
Réceptionniste	Oui. Qu'est-ce que vous voulez comme chambre?
Client	Une chambre avec salle de bains.
Réceptionniste	Pour combien de personnes?
Client	Pour une personne.
Réceptionniste	Et pour combien de nuits?
Client	Une nuit seulement.
Réceptionniste	Très bien.
Client	C'est combien, la chambre?
Réceptionniste	600 francs la chambre, plus 55 francs le petit déjeuner.
Client	D'accord.
Réceptionniste	Je vais vous donner la chambre seize. C'est la troisième porte à gauche.

a. Est-ce que l'hôtel a des chambres pour ce soir? ....

b. Qu'est-ce que le client désire comme chambre?

....

c. La chambre est pour combien de personnes? ....

d. Le client reste combien de nuits? ....

e. C'est combien, la chambre? ....

f. Où est la chambre 16? ....

Exercise 4

Now write in the blanks what you would say to the receptionist if you wanted

- a room for tonight
- with shower
- for two people
- for three nights

When you have done all that, ask how much the room is.

Vous Bonjour, Monsieur.

Réceptionniste Bonjour, Messieurs-dames.

Vous ....

Réceptionniste Oui. Qu'est-ce que vous voulez comme chambre?

Vous ....

Réceptionniste D'accord. Pour combien de personnes?

Vous ....

Réceptionniste Et pour combien de nuits?

Vous ....

Réceptionniste Très bien.

Vous ....

Réceptionniste 630 francs par nuit, plus le petit déjeuner.

Exercise 5   You are with a group of Americans who do not speak French. The hotel desk clerk does not speak English, so you need to give everybody's room number in order for them to get their keys. The number is usually preceded by **la**, because either **la clé** or **la chambre** is understood. For example, 'Twenty-one, please' is **La vingt et un, s'il vous plaît**. How will you ask for these keys?

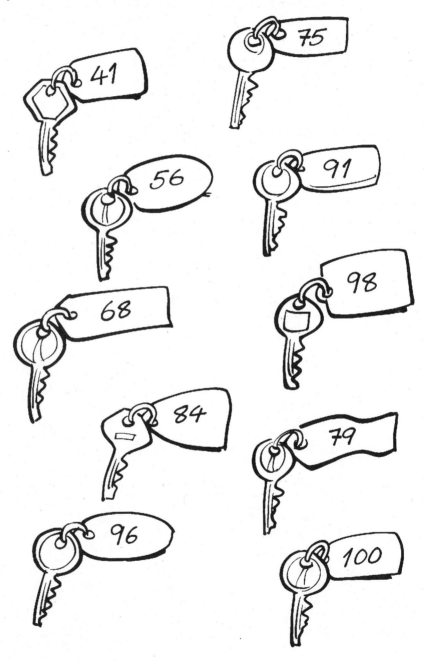

Exercise 6   Hidden in the word square are the French words for:

letter	to the right	black	seventy-six
to confirm	all booked (plural)	man	first
bathroom	to sell	week	how many
time	(I) understand	spaces	certainly
last name	toilets	days	to give
two expressions meaning 'sorry'			

The French words are written across (left-to-right) or down, and many of the letters are used in more than one word. Can you circle them all?

A	S	A	L	L	E	D	E	B	A	I	N	S
R	J	T	T	W	K	L	M	I	E	E	C	O
P	L	S	E	M	A	I	N	E	A	B	E	I
P	O	L	M	H	G	A	S	N	O	M	Q	X
C	O	M	P	R	E	N	D	S	F	G	D	A
O	P	L	S	A	N	O	D	U	S	J	O	N
M	E	T	V	Y	O	I	T	R	N	O	N	T
P	R	E	M	I	E	R	W	D	T	U	N	E
L	A	D	R	O	I	T	E	P	O	R	E	S
E	X	C	U	S	E	Z	M	O	I	S	R	E
T	P	A	R	D	O	N	A	M	L	N	N	I
S	D	C	O	N	F	I	R	M	E	R	L	Z
C	O	M	B	I	E	N	A	T	T	E	N	E
H	O	M	M	E	L	L	E	T	T	R	E	V
A	B	L	M	V	E	N	D	R	E	A	N	D
P	E	M	R	P	L	A	C	E	S	A	W	E

ANSWERS

Exercise 1

Est-ce que vous avez des chambres pour ce soir? / Oui, nous avons des chambres.
Combien de chambres voulez-vous? / Deux chambres d'une personne.
Pour combien de temps? / Pour deux nuits.
Avec salle de bains? / Non, avec cabinet de toilette.
Où est la clé? / Dans la chambre.

Exercise 2

a. changer / chèques **b.** chambre / cabinet **c.** comprends
d. confirmer **e.** combien

Exercise 3

a. oui **b.** une chambre avec salle de bains **c.** pour une personne
d. une nuit **e.** 600 francs (plus 55 francs le petit déjeuner)
f. la troisième porte à gauche

Exercise 4

Your wording may be correct without necessarily being exactly the same as this:
Vous avez une chambre pour ce soir, s'il vous plaît? / Une chambre avec douche. / (Pour) deux personnes. / (Pour) trois nuits. / C'est combien (la chambre)?

Exercise 5

41 – La quarante et un, s'il vous plaît. / 56 – La cinquante-six, s'il vous plaît. / 68 – La soixante-huit, s'il vous plaît. / 84 – La quatre-vingt-quatre, s'il vous plaît. / 96 – La quatre-vingt-seize, s'il vous plaît. / 75 – La soixante-quinze, s'il vous plaît. / 91 – La quatre-vingt-onze, s'il vous plaît. / 98 – La quatre-vingt-dix-huit, s'il vous plaît. / 79 – La soixante-dix-neuf, s'il vous plaît. / 100 – La cent, s'il vous plaît.

Exercise 6

A	S	A	L	L	E	D	E	B	A	I	N	S
R	J	T	T	W	K	L	M	I	E	E	C	O
P	L	S	E	M	A	I	N	E	A	B	E	I
P	O	L	M	H	G	A	S	N	O	M	Q	X
C	O	M	P	R	E	N	D	S	F	G	D	A
O	P	L	S	A	N	O	D	U	S	J	O	N
M	E	T	V	Y	O	I	T	R	N	O	N	T
P	R	E	M	I	E	R	W	D	T	U	N	E
L	A	D	R	O	I	T	E	P	O	R	E	S
E	X	C	U	S	E	Z	M	O	I	S	R	E
T	P	A	R	D	O	N	A	M	L	N	N	I
S	D	C	O	N	F	I	R	M	E	R	L	Z
C	O	M	B	I	E	N	A	T	T	E	N	E
H	O	M	M	E	L	L	E	T	T	R	E	V
A	B	L	M	V	E	N	D	R	E	A	N	D
P	E	M	R	P	L	A	C	E	S	A	W	E

5 DIRECTIONS

Exercise 1   Which preposition belongs in which blank?

pour	sous	en face de	à côté de
	sur	derrière	

a. **La clé est** .... **la table.**

d. **C'est** .... **vous.**

b. **Ils dansent** .... **le pont.**

e. **Jean est** .... **Marie.**

c. **Chez les éléphants, l'enfant marche**
.... **la mère.**

(**chez** here means 'among' or 'in the kingdom of')

f. **Jean est** .... **Marie.**

Exercise 2   You are going to a conference that is being held in a French university dormitory (**une résidence universitaire**). You ask a French colleague **Pour aller à la résidence?** and you are given the following directions from downtown:

> **Du centre-ville, vous prenez la direction de Paris. Vous traversez le Pont St-Michel. Après le pont, vous prenez la troisième à droite, et puis vous tournez à gauche. Vous allez tout droit pendant deux cents mètres et puis vous trouverez la résidence universitaire sur votre gauche.**

If the directions are correct, which of the buildings 1–8 on the map is the dormitory?

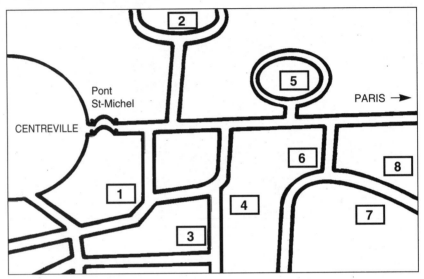

Exercise 3   You are the first to arrive at the dormitory and are immediately recruited to help the busy organizer of the conference. You are asked to find out from the janitor (**le/la concierge**) where the various amenities are and then write a sign to tell the participants. Here is your conversation with the janitor. Read it through at least three times before you go on to write the sign.

Concierge	Vous parlez français?
Vous	Un petit peu.
Concierge	Alors, les douches sont au premier étage et au troisième étage.
Vous	D'accord.

Concierge	Les toilettes pour les messieurs sont au rez-de-chaussée et au deuxième étage, et les toilettes pour les dames sont au premier et au troisième.
Vous	Bien.
Concierge	Au rez-de-chaussée, vous avez une cafétéria, et au sous-sol il y a un bar.
Vous	Pardon – c'est quoi, le sous-sol?
Concierge	Eh bien, vous avez le troisième étage, le deuxième étage, le premier étage, le rez-de-chaussée, et puis *(pointing downwards)* le sous-sol.
Vous	Ah d'accord – je comprends. Et où sont les téléphones, s'il vous plaît?
Concierge	Au sous-sol, à côté du bar. Et puis il y a des machines à laver, également au sous-sol.
Vous	Pardon. Des machines à laver, qu'est-ce que c'est?
Concierge	C'est 'washing machines' en anglais, je pense.
Vous	Ah d'accord, merci.

Now for your sign, which needs to be written in French.
Fill in the amenities by the appropriate floor number.
RC = Rez-de-chaussée (ground floor)
SS = Sous-sol (basement)

3^e	
2^e	
1er	
RC	
SS	

Exercise 4   Some of the participants want to go out to the restaurant which is marked on the map on page 26 as number 2. Assuming that you have pointed them in the right direction to start with, can you give them directions from the dormitory? The framework below should help you. (The words **ensuite** and **puis** both mean 'then'.)

a.   **Vous allez** ....

b.   **Vous prenez la** .... **à** ....

c.   **Ensuite, vous prenez la** .... **à** .... :

    c'est dans la direction du ....

d.   **Vous prenez la** .... **à** .... **et puis la**

    .... **à** ....

e.   **Et là, vous trouverez le restaurant sur votre** ....

Exercise 5

a.   See if you can trace these two sets of directions on the map of the Paris métro:

Touriste   Pour aller à Montmartre, s'il vous plaît?
Parisien   De l'Étoile, vous prenez le métro, direction Nation, et vous descendez à Anvers.

Touriste   Pour aller à la gare Montparnasse?
Parisien   De l'Étoile, vous prenez la direction Château de Vincennes. Il faut changer à Champs Élysées Clemenceau. Là, vous prenez la direction Châtillon-Montrouge et vous descendez à Montparnasse Bienvenüe.

b.   Now say aloud, or write on a separate piece of paper, how you would give those directions to a child (whom you would call **tu**).

Vous
êtes ici.
⇨

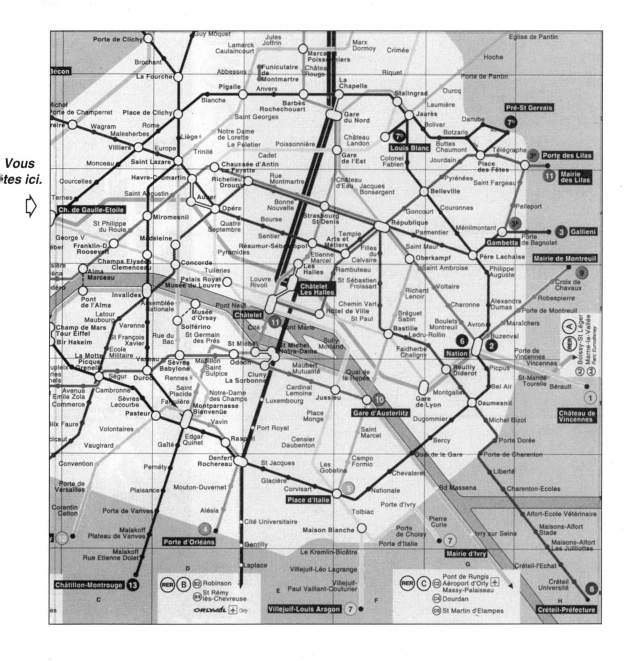

Exercise 6   French friends have sent you these directions to their house.
Can you translate them for your partner, who does not
understand French?

Du centre - ville, vous prenez la direction de QUIMPER.
Vous passez devant la cathédrale et vous faites un
kilomètre. Là, vous avez l'église ST. PAUL sur votre
droite. Vous continuez tout droit et puis vous prenez la
deuxième à gauche après l'église _ c'est la rue
MAZARIN. Ensuite, c'est la première à droite _ c'est la
rue GILBERT. Nous sommes à 300 mètres sur la
gauche.

....

....

....

....

....

....

....

....

....

....

ANSWERS

Exercise 1

a. sous **b.** sur **c.** derrière **d.** pour **e.** à côté de **f.** en face de

Exercise 2

8

Exercise 3

3ᵉ	toilettes – dames; douches
2ᵉ	toilettes – messieurs
1ᵉʳ	toilettes – dames; douches
RC	cafétéria; toilettes – messieurs
SS	bar; téléphones; machines à laver

Exercise 4

a. tout droit **b.** première / droite **c.** première / gauche / centre-ville
d. deuxième / droite / première / droite **e.** gauche

Exercise 5

a You should have started from l'Étoile and followed the métro line in the direction of Nation, as far as Anvers.
You should again have started from l'Étoile and followed the métro line in the direction of Château de Vincennes, changed at Champs Élysées Clemenceau and followed the line in the direction of Châtillon-Montrouge as far as Montparnasse Bienvenüe.

b. Montmartre: De l'Étoile, tu prends le métro, direction Nation, et tu descends à Anvers.
La gare Montparnasse: De l'Étoile, tu prends la direction Château de Vincennes. Il faut changer à Champs Élysées Clemenceau. Là, tu prends la direction Châtillon-Montrouge et tu descends à Montparnasse Bienvenüe.

Exercise 6

A literal translation would run: From downtown, you take the Quimper direction. You pass in front of the cathedral and you go one kilometer. There, you have St. Paul's church on your right. You continue straight ahead and then you take the second on the left after the church – that is the rue Mazarin. Then it's the first on the right – that's the rue Gilbert. We are 300 meters along on the left.

Exercise 1   Can you put these events in chronological order?

a. J'arrive au bureau vers neuf heures moins le quart. ☐

b. Nous prenons le petit déjeuner à huit heures moins dix. ☐

c. Les enfants vont à l'école à huit heures et demie. ☐

d. Je prends une douche vers sept heures. ☐

e. Mon travail commence à neuf heures. ☐

f. Les enfants ont la salle de bains de sept heures et quart à huit heures moins le quart. ☐

Exercise 2   One evening you find that everybody's watch says something different. Here are the times that people give you. Which of them are within five minutes of the correct time of 9:30?

a. Il est dix heures moins le quart. ☐

b. Il est dix heures moins vingt-cinq. ☐

c. Il est vingt et une heures vingt-neuf. ☐

d. Il est vingt et une heures trente-sept. ☐

e. Il est neuf heures et demie. ☐

f. Il est vingt-deux heures trente. ☐

Exercise 3 Can you write out the times shown, assuming that they are all
P.M.? It does not matter whether you use the 12-hour or the
24-hour system. (For the first one, for example, you can write
either **Il est onze heures et demie** or **Il est vingt-trois heures
trente.**)

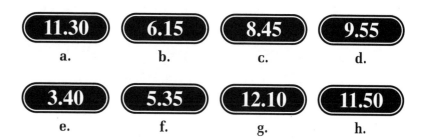

11.30	**6.15**	**8.45**	**9.55**
a.	b.	c.	d.
3.40	**5.35**	**12.10**	**11.50**
e.	f.	g.	h.

a. ....

b. ....

c. ....

d. ....

e. ....

f. ....

g. ....

h. ....

Exercise 4 Fill in the French names for the days of the week. 1 = Monday,
2 = Tuesday, etc.

Exercise 5   This time, fill in the names of the months. 1 = January, 2 = February, etc. (Note: in the grid, 1 = down, 7 = across.)

Exercise 6   See if you can match up the questions and the answers.

a.   Quelle heure est-il?

b.   A quelle heure est-ce que le train part?

c.   Il est en retard?

d.   Ça fait combien?

e.   De quelle heure à quelle heure est-ce que c'est ouvert?

1   356 francs.

2   A dix-neuf heures trente-neuf.

3   Il est dix-neuf heures.

4   De sept heures du matin à onze heures du soir.

5   Oui.

Exercise 7 French friends ask the birthdays of all your family. Write out in full how you would tell them, following the model of the first one.

Michael: March 27   **L'anniversaire de Michael, c'est le vingt-sept mars.**

Gerard: May 14   ....

Greg: January 1   ....

Barbara: August 13   ....

Marianne: April 3   ....

Peter: July 1   ....

Liz: February 14   ....

Exercise 8 You are writing a card to French friends to encourage them to come and visit you – preferably while your children are on vacation from school. See if you can add to the card, in French, the information that the children are on vacation:

from December 20 to January 6   from February 25 to March 1
from April 8 to 23   from May 24 to June 1
from July 22 to September 7   from October 29 to November 3

Remember that 'from ... to' is **de ... à**. And remember what happens when **de** or **à** is followed by **le**:

de + le → du   **à + le → au**

The usual way of writing **premier** in figures is 1er.

Merci beaucoup de la carte de Biarritz. Oui, venez en Angleterre! Les enfants sont en vacances:
du 20 décembre au 6 janvier

....

....

....

....

....

Venez quand vous voulez!

ANSWERS

Exercise 1
a. 5 **b.** 3 **c.** 4 **d.** 1 **e.** 6 **f.** 2

Exercise 2
b, c, e

Exercise 3
a. Il est onze heures et demie. OR Il est vingt-trois heures trente.
b. Il est six heures et quart. OR Il est dix-huit heures quinze.
c. Il est neuf heures moins le quart. OR Il est vingt heures quarante-cinq.
d. Il est dix heures moins cinq. OR Il est vingt et une heures cinquante-cinq.
e. Il est quatre heures moins vingt. OR Il est quinze heures quarante.
f. Il est six heures moins vingt-cinq. OR Il est dix-sept heures trente-cinq.
g. Il est midi dix. OR Il est douze heures dix.
h. Il est minuit moins dix. OR Il est vingt-trois heures cinquante.

Exercise 4   **Exercise 5**

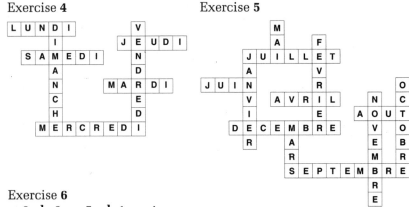

Exercise 6
a. 3 **b.** 2 **c.** 5 **d.** 1 **e.** 4

Exercise 7
L'anniversaire de Gerard, c'est le quatorze mai. / L'anniversaire de Greg, c'est le premier janvier. / L'anniversaire de Barbara, c'est le treize août. / L'anniversaire de Marianne, c'est le trois avril. / L'anniversaire de Peter, c'est le premier juillet. / L'anniversaire de Liz, c'est le quatorze février.

Exercise 8
du 20 décembre au 6 janvier; du 25 février au 1er mars; du 8 au 23 avril; du 24 mai au 1er juin; du 22 juillet au 7 septembre; du 29 octobre au 3 novembre

7 SHOPPING (part 1)

Exercise 1   Circle the one that doesn't belong in each of these sets of words.

      a.   **veau / cheval / chou / volaille**

      b.   **agneau / pommes de terre / petits pois / carottes**

      c.   **pomme / poire / melon / poisson**

      d.   **kilos / baguettes / grammes / livres**

      e.   **boîte / raisin / bouteille / paquet**

      f.   **États-Unis / américain / Washington / rendez-vous**

Exercise 2   Which of these expressions of quantity would you be most likely to use in buying each of the items on the shopping list below?

      a.   **Une livre de ...**
      b.   **Une bouteille de ...**
      c.   **Un paquet de ...**
      d.   **Une boîte de ...**
      e.   **100 grammes de ...**
      f.   **Six ...**

      1   **œufs**
      2   **sardines**
      3   **sucre**
      4   **vin**
      5   **pâté**
      6   **tomates**

Exercise 3   Can you write out these prices in figures?

Example   **deux cent trente-deux francs**: 232F

It is also often written 232,00. (The zeros after the comma refer to **centimes**.)

a.   **trois cent soixante-treize francs** ....

b.   **quatre cent quinze francs** ....

c.   **six cent soixante et onze francs** ....

d.   **sept cent soixante-dix-sept francs** ....

e.   **huit cent quatre-vingt-un francs** ....

f.   **neuf cent quatre-vingt-seize francs** ....

Exercise 4   Now can you write these prices out in words?

Example   **55,00F**:   **cinquante-cinq francs**

a.   79,00 ....

b.   81,00 ....

c.   93,00 ....

d.   376,00 ....

e.   692,00 ....

f.   717,00 ....

g.   999,00 ....

h.   1000,00 ....

Exercise 5   Underline the correct forms of the adjectives in brackets in the following conversation between a salesperson and a customer. (Note: **fait** is used to mean 'ripe' when referring to cheese.)

Commerçant   Bonjour, Madame.

Cliente   Bonjour, Monsieur. Je voudrais une bouteille de vin [blanc/blanche/blancs/blanches], s'il vous plaît. Vous avez du Muscadet?

Commerçant   Oui, bien sûr, Madame. Voilà: un [bon/bonne/bons/bonnes] [petit/petite/petits/petites] Muscadet de Sèvre-et-Maine.

Cliente   Merci. Et puis, je voudrais un camembert bien [fait/faite/faits/faites], s'il vous plaît.

Commerçant   D'accord ... voilà.

Cliente   Et puis cinq bananes.

Commerçant   Voilà.

Cliente   Mais ces bananes sont [noir/noire/noirs/noires]!

Commerçant   Elles sont très [mûr/mûre/mûrs/mûres], effectivement.

Cliente   Alors, je ne prends pas de bananes. Vous me donnez un kilo de pommes, s'il vous plaît.

Commerçant   Des [petit/petite/petits/petites] ou des [gros/grosse/gros/grosses], Madame?

Cliente   Des [gros/grosse/gros/grosses], s'il vous plaît.

Commerçant   Voilà. Ce sera tout?

Cliente   Oui, ce sera tout. Merci.

A market stall in Old Nice

Exercise 6   Here are some ads for grocery stores on the Rhuys peninsula (**la presqu'île de Rhuys**) in Brittany. You won't know all the words in them, but see if you can understand enough to answer the questions.

Alimentations

BOULANGERIE - PATISSERIE - CONFISERIE

R. JOUAN   **A LA GOURMANDISE**

Pain à l'ancienne sur boulenc
Spécialités bretonnes « le Goth »
Chocolats maison - Glaces maison

5, rue Général de Gaulle, 56730 ST-GILDAS-DE-RHUYS, Tél. 97 45 23 37

SUPERMARCHÉ
Chemin du Puits David (Face Parking Municipal)
ST-GILDAS-DE-RHUYS – Tél. 97.45.24.86

B O U L A N G E R I E
P A T I S S E R I E
C R Ê P E R I E
J. LAYEC
20, rue du Gal de Gaulle
SARZEAU - ☎ 97 41 71 90
5 place Richemont
SARZEAU - ☎ 97 41 79 01

PATISSERIE-BOULANGERIE
CONFISERIE
C. RIVIÈRE
2 place Richemont
SARZEAU
Tél. 97 41 78 04

Poissonnerie LE FUR
5 RUE DU GENERAL DE GAULLE - SARZEAU
TÉL. 97.41.83.51
Arrivage journalier de POISSONS
de chalutiers et de petits bateaux des PORTS DE
LORIENT et QUIBERON Vivier de crustacés et homards
Aquarium de poissons du pays

a.   How many of these stores are bakeries?

....

b.   Which one is also a pancake house?

....

c.   What is the name of the supermarket?

....

d.   What is the French word for 'fish store'?

....

e.   Which store advertises its ice cream?

....

f.   Which shop is on a street across from the city parking lot?

....

Exercise 7   When you are in France, it is a good idea to write your shopping list in French, so that you know what to ask for when you are in the store. Try this one, writing out **un/une** in full to remind yourself of the genders.

a chicken	....
a bottle of wine	....
a pound of butter	....
four bananas	....
a kilo of apples	....
a can of sardines	....
a box of sugar	....

Exercise 8   If you needed to make an appointment with a doctor in France, this is the sort of conversation you might have with the receptionist. Can write the correct words in the blanks? You may not know the words **aujourd'hui** (today) and **demain** (tomorrow).

complet	fille	rendez-vous	heures	heure
nom	**voudrais**	**aujourd'hui**	**demain**	

Réceptionniste   Bonjour, Monsieur. Vous désirez?

Jack   Bonjour, Madame. Je .... un .... avec le médecin, s'il vous plaît.

Réceptionniste   Oui, pour quel jour?

Jack   .... si possible.

Réceptionniste   Ah non, aujourd'hui c'est .... , si vous voulez?

Jack   Oui – à quelle .... ?

Réceptionniste   A onze .... ?

Jack   Très bien. A onze heures demain, alors.

Réceptionniste   Vous pouvez me donner votre .... , s'il vous plaît?

Jack   Le rendez-vous est pour ma .... , Elizabeth James.

Réceptionniste   Elizabeth James. D'accord.

ANSWERS

Exercise **1**
a. chou (the rest are all meat) **b.** agneau (the rest are all vegetables)
c. poisson (the rest are all fruit) **d.** baguettes (the rest are all units
of weight) **e.** raisin (the rest are all containers) **f.** rendez-vous (the
rest all have something to do with the USA)

Exercise **2**
a. 6 **b.** 4 **c.** 3 **d.** 2 **e.** 5 **f.** 1

Exercise **3**
a. 373F **b.** 415F **c.** 671F **d.** 777F **e.** 881F **f.** 996F

Exercise **4**
a. soixante-dix-neuf francs **b.** quatre-vingt-un francs **c.** quatre-
vingt-treize francs **d.** trois cent soixante-seize francs **e.** six cent
quatre-vingt-douze francs **f.** sept cent dix-sept francs **g.** neuf cent
quatre-vingt-dix-neuf francs **h.** mille francs

Exercise **5**
blanc / bon / petit / fait / noires / mûres / petites / grosses / grosses

Exercise **6**
a. 3 **b.** J. Layec **c.** Comod **d.** poissonnerie **e.** A la Gourmandise
f. Comod

Exercise **7**
un poulet; une bouteille de vin; une livre de beurre; quatre bananes;
un kilo de pommes; une boîte de sardines; un paquet de sucre

Exercise **8**
voudrais; rendez-vous; aujourd'hui; complet; demain; heure;
heures; nom; fille

Exercise 1   Study the word square and see if you can circle French words for:

hat	jacket	sweater
tie	scarf	shirt
pants	shorts	skirt
dress	slip	bra
tights	stocking	sock
shoe	underpants	bathing suit

C	R	A	V	A	T	E	R	S	F	J	H	A
H	N	P	E	D	S	J	O	J	O	B	A	S
A	R	U	S	V	A	U	B	L	U	E	N	T
U	I	L	T	N	E	P	E	S	L	I	P	C
S	S	L	E	D	A	O	Y	H	A	I	M	O
S	O	U	T	I	E	N	G	O	R	G	E	L
E	C	H	E	M	I	S	E	R	D	I	J	L
T	C	H	A	P	E	A	U	T	S	S	U	A
T	Y	C	H	A	U	S	S	U	R	E	P	N
E	O	P	A	N	T	A	L	O	N	U	E	T
M	A	I	L	L	O	T	D	E	B	A	I	N

The French words are written across (left-to-right) or down; a number of the letters are used in more than one word.

Exercise 2

Mais oui, Madame ...

A. Ce magnifique manteau est à 999F!
100% laine
Couleurs: noir, bleu marine, vert foncé, rouge
Tailles: 38–48

B. Ce charmant petit chemisier à fleurs est à
seulement 399F!
100% soie
Couleurs: bleu clair/bleu foncé, rose/bleu
marine, jaune/marron
Tailles: 38–50

C. Cette jupe élégante est à 449F!
100% acrylique
Couleurs: marron, gris, rose foncé
Tailles: 38–48

Mais oui, Monsieur ...

D. Cette belle veste est à seulement 899F!
50% laine, 40% acrylique, 10% nylon
Couleurs: noir, gris clair, rouge
Tailles: 48–56

E. Ce pull (j'♥!) est à 449F!
60% laine, 40% acrylique
Couleurs: marron/bleu clair, rouge/bleu,
rose/gris
Tailles: 46–58

F. Ce pantalon élégant mais confortable est
à 399F!
60% coton, 40% polyester
Couleurs: noir, bleu marine, vert foncé
Tailles: 50–56

Bon de commande

NOM .... ADRESSE ....

.... NUMÉRO DE TÉLÉPHONE ....

ARTICLE	QUANTITÉ	COULEUR	TAILLE	PRIX

See if you can fill in the order form (**le bon de commande**) to order:

1 coat in black: size 44
1 blouse in pink/navy: size 44
1 skirt in grey: size 44
1 jacket in red: size 54
1 sweater in brown/light blue: size 54
1 pair of pants in dark green: size 54

Note   You say **Le pantalon est gris** but **La jupe est grise**. However, on a form like this, you can write either **gris** or **grise** as the color for **la jupe**. The logic behind this is that you can ask either for **une jupe grise** or for **une jupe en gris**.

Exercise 3   Which of these phrases belongs in each of the blanks? (Remember that **trop** means 'too ...' and **plus ... que** means 'more ... than' – and look to see whether the clothes being described are masculine or feminine, singular or plural.)

plus petit	plus petite	plus petits	plus petites
	trop petit	trop petite	trop petits

a.   **Ce maillot de bain est** ....

b.   **Cette robe est** ....

c.   **Ces vêtements sont** ....

d.   **La chemise blanche est** .... **que la chemise noire.**

e.   **Les chaussettes blanches sont** .... **que les chaussettes noires.**

f.   **Le manteau noir est** .... **que le manteau blanc.**

g.   **Les bas blancs sont** .... **que les bas noirs.**

Exercise 4   Here are the stores in an arcade.

ALIMENTATION	**LIBRAIRIE**
BANQUE	**MODE FÉMININE**
PARFUMERIE	**PHARMACIE**
CONFISERIE	**TABAC**

And here is your shopping list. Which of the things on it are you *unlikely* to find in these stores?

du saucisson   des chocolats
une robe   des chèques de voyage
la Bible   des timbres
des fleurs   de l'aspirine
de l'eau de toilette

Exercise 5   Our friend here is full of aches and pains. Can you write each of his complaints in the appropriate spaces?

J'ai mal au dos.   J'ai mal aux pieds.   J'ai mal à la gorge.
J'ai mal à la tête.   J'ai mal au ventre.   J'ai mal aux dents.

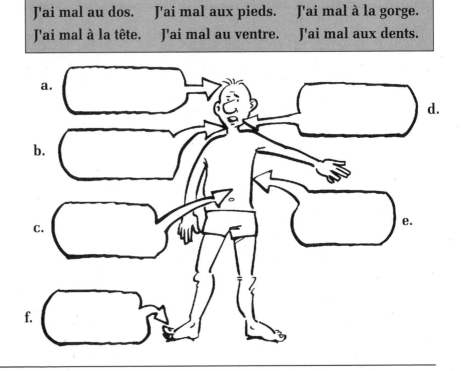

a.

b.

c.

d.

e.

f.

Exercise 6 Here is the skeleton of a conversation between a pharmacist and a customer. The customer's lines are given in the box, out of order. Can you write them out in the correct blanks?

> **En comprimés.**   **Oui – c'est pour moi.**
>
> **Je voudrais aussi quelque chose contre la diarrhée.**
>
> **Bonjour, Madame. Vous avez quelque chose contre le mal de tête, s'il vous plaît?**
>
> **D'accord.**   **Oui, ce sera tout. Merci.**
>
> **Ah non, je ne peux pas prendre d'aspirine.**

Pharmacienne Bonjour, Monsieur.

Client ....

....

Pharmacienne Vous voulez de l'aspirine?

Client ....

Pharmacienne Du paracétamol, alors?

Client ....

Pharmacienne En comprimés ou en suppositoires?

Client ....

Pharmacienne Voilà. Ce sera tout?

Client ....

Pharmacienne C'est pour un adulte?

Client ....

Pharmacienne Voilà. Ce sera tout?

Client ....

Exercise 1

C	R	A	V	A	T	E	R	S	F	J	H	A
H	N	P	E	D	S	J	O	J	O	B	A	S
A	R	U	S	V	A	U	B	L	U	E	N	T
U	I	L	T	N	E	P	E	S	L	I	P	C
S	S	L	E	D	A	O	Y	H	A	I	M	O
S	O	U	T	I	E	N	G	O	R	G	E	L
E	C	H	E	M	I	S	E	R	D	I	J	L
T	C	H	A	P	E	A	U	T	S	S	U	A
T	Y	C	H	A	U	S	S	U	R	E	P	N
E	O	P	A	N	T	A	L	O	N	U	E	T
M	A	I	L	L	O	T	D	E	B	A	I	N

Exercise 2

ARTICLE	QUANTITÉ	COULEUR	TAILLE	PRIX
Manteau	1	noir	44	999F
Chemisier	1	rose/bleu marine	44	399F
Jupe	1	gris(e)	44	449F
Veste	1	rouge	54	899F
Pullover	1	marron/bleu clair	54	449F
Pantalon	1	vert foncé	54	399F

Exercise 3

a. Ce maillot de bain est trop petit. **b.** Cette robe est trop petite.
c. Ces vêtements sont trop petits. **d.** La chemise blanche est plus petite que la chemise noire. **e.** Les chaussettes blanches sont plus petites que les chaussettes noires. **f.** Le manteau noir est plus petit que le manteau blanc. **g.** Les bas blancs sont plus petits que les bas noirs.

Exercise 4

des fleurs

Exercise 5

a. J'ai mal à la tête. **b.** J'ai mal à la gorge. **c.** J'ai mal au ventre.
d. J'ai mal aux dents. **e.** J'ai mal au dos. **f.** J'ai mal aux pieds.

Exercise 6

Bonjour, Madame. Vous avez quelque chose contre le mal de tête, s'il vous plaît? / Ah non, je ne peux pas prendre d'aspirine. / D'accord. / En comprimés. / Je voudrais aussi quelque chose contre la diarrhée. / Oui – c'est pour moi. / Oui, ce sera tout. Merci.

Exercise 1   Here is a letter from a French friend who is coming to stay with you.

> Saint-Aignan
> le 4 juin
>
> Chers amis,
>
> Bonjour de Saint-Aignan !
> Merci de votre lettre. Oui j'ai mon billet.
> Je prends donc l'avion de Paris-Charles
> de Gaulle à midi le dimanche 5 juillet
> et j'arrive à J.F.K. à 15h magique,
> non ! C'est un vol Air France
> (numéro AF 973). Qu'est-ce que je dois
> faire pour aller chez vous ?
> Est-ce qu'il y a un train ? Ou
> est-ce que vous pouvez venir me
> chercher à l'aéroport ?
>
> A bientôt
> Catherine

a.   Does she have her ticket yet?

....

b.   On which day of the week and date is she coming?

....

c.   What time is her flight due in at JFK?

....

d.   Why does she jokingly describe the flight times as magic?

....

e.   What do you need to write and tell her?

....

....

Exercise 2   All the answers to the crossword are words that you may need when traveling.

Across

6	Information (14)
9	Is it **le** or **la prix**? (2)
10	Subway (5)
13	Some (2)
14	Bed (3)
15	Toll/tollgate (5)
18	To prefer (8)
19	On the top: **en** ... (4)
21	Baggage check (8)
25	Platform (4)
26	Is it **le** or **la couverture**? (2)
28	In (2)
30	Soap (5)
31	Bus station: 16 down ... (8)
33	Way in (6)
34	Full (5)
36	On (3)

Down

1	First class (8, 6)
2	Says (3)
3	(They) have (3)
4	Friend (3)
5	Tire (4)
7	Way out (6)
8	Under (4)
11	And (2)
12	Abroad: **à** ... (1, 8)
16	Station (4)
17	Bag (3)
20	Lost and Found: **objets** ... (7)
22	Negative (2)
23	He (2)
24	Suitcase (6)
27	Your (5)
29	Our (3)
32	Some (3)
35	Is it **le** or **la drap**? (2)

Exercise 3 Can you match up the phrases from the two columns to make possible sentences?

a. **Le train est**   1   **voyager en couchette.**
b. **Les trains sont**   2   **aller simple?**
c. **Les couchettes sont**   3   **moins chers que les bus.**
d. **Vous pouvez**   4   **moins cher que le bus.**
e. **C'est un billet aller et** 5 **moins chères que les voitures-**
   retour ou   **lits.**

Exercise 4 See if you can write the words and phrases from the box in the blanks of this conversation at a station ticket counter:

places	demain	quel	deuxième	réservation	cher
aller et retour		Fumeurs?	Non-fumeurs	reste	

Employé   Madame?

Cliente   Bonjour, Monsieur. Je voudrais un .... pour Béziers, s'il vous plaît.

Employé   En .... classe?

Cliente   Oui, oui. Et avec une ....

Employé   Pour quel jour?

Cliente   Pour ....

Employé   Et pour .... train?

Cliente   Le train de 17h 47.

Employé   .... Non-fumeurs?

Cliente   ....

Employé   (*vérifie*) Ah! Il ne reste plus de .... non-fumeurs en deuxième classe.

Cliente   Aïe! C'est beaucoup plus .... en première classe?

Employé   C'est 50% plus cher.

Cliente   Et il vous .... des places non-fumeurs en première classe?

Employé   (*vérifie*) Oui, Madame.

Cliente   Allez! Je prends un billet de première classe.

Exercise 5   Here is the schedule of trains from Tours to Caen. To follow it, you will need to understand the words **circuler** (to run), **tous les jours** (every day), **sauf** (except), **fêtes** (public holidays) and the abbreviations for days of the week **lun (lundi)**, **sam (samedi)** and **dim (dimanche)**.

Tours ▷ Caen					265 km
Les trains circulent	Départ ▼	Arrivée ▼	Changement	No	Places – services offerts
● les lun sauf le 31 mai; ● le 1er juin.	03.58	06.58		13030	1.2
● les dim et fêtes.	09.05	12.47	Le Mans 10.24/10.53	87106 13033	1.2 🚲 1.2
● tous les jours sauf les dim et fêtes.	09.38	12.47		13032	1.2
● tous les jours.	15.14	18.04		13034	1.2
● tous les jours sauf les ven, sam et sauf le 30 mai.	16.56	20.04		13036	1.2
● les ven.	16.56	20.06		13036	1.2
● les ven, dim et fêtes sauf les 30 mai et 14 juil.	20.08	22.54		13038	1.2 🚲

a.   What is the earliest you can arrive in Caen on a Wednesday?

....

b.   What is the latest departure from Tours on a Saturday?

....

c.   Why is the 9:05 slower than the 9:38?

....

d.   On what day of the week must May 31 have fallen in the year

of this schedule? ....

Exercise 6   How would you ask these questions in French?

a.   Does the 16:56 train run every day?

....

b.   Do you have the times for coming back from Caen?

....

c.   Is it necessary to change?

....

d.   What time does the 15:14 train arrive in Caen?

....

e.   Which platform is it?

....

*A TGV Sud-Est train
in Annecy station*

ANSWERS

Exercise 1

a. Yes **b.** Sunday July 5 **c.** 12 noon **d.** Because the departure and arrival times are so close (owing to the time difference between France and the U.S.). **e.** How to get to your house from the airport (whether there is a train or whether you will meet her).

Exercise 2

	P				D		O		A		P			
	R	E	N	S	E	I	G	N	E	M	E	N	T	S
L	E			O		T		T		I		E		O
	M	E	T	R	O		L				D	U		U
L	I	T		P	E	A	G	E						S
	E		I		T		A				S			
P	R	E	F	E	R	E	R		R		H	A	U	T
	E					A		E			C			R
	C	O	N	S	I	G	N	E		V				O
	L		E		L		G		Q	U	A	I		U
L	A		V		E	N			L					V
	S	A	V	O	N		R	O	U	T	I	E	R	E
	S		T		D		S			S				S
	E	N	T	R	E	E		P	L	E	I	N		
			E		S	U	R		E					

Exercise 3

a. 4 **b.** 3 **c.** 5 **d.** 1 **e.** 2

Exercise 4

Bonjour, Monsieur. Je voudrais un aller et retour pour Béziers, s'il vous plaît. / En deuxième classe? / Oui, oui. Et avec une réservation. / Pour demain. / Et pour quel train? / Fumeurs? Non-fumeurs? / Non-fumeurs. / Ah! Il ne reste plus de places non-fumeurs en deuxième classe. / Aïe! C'est beaucoup plus cher en première classe? / Et il vous reste des places non-fumeurs en première classe?

Exercise 5

a. 12:47 **b.** 15:14 **c.** Because you have to change at Le Mans. **d.** Monday (because the first entry on the schedule reads 'Mondays except for May 31').

Exercise 6

a. Est-ce que le train de 16h 56 circule tous les jours? **b.** Est-ce que vous avez les horaires pour revenir de Caen? **c.** Est-ce qu'il faut changer? **d.** A quelle heure est-ce que le train de 15h 14 arrive à Caen? **e.** C'est quel quai?

Exercise 1 Which of these items are inedible?

un œuf   des rillettes

une addition   du jambon

une côte de porc   un verre

des pommes frites   des radis

un chou-fleur   une cuillère

un croque-monsieur   des gens

Exercise 2   Menus often feature a cover-charge (**le couvert**). Can you label some of the items which **le couvert** would include? One of them has been done for you. (Note: In France it is usual to put the glass in the middle rather than to the right of the place-setting.)

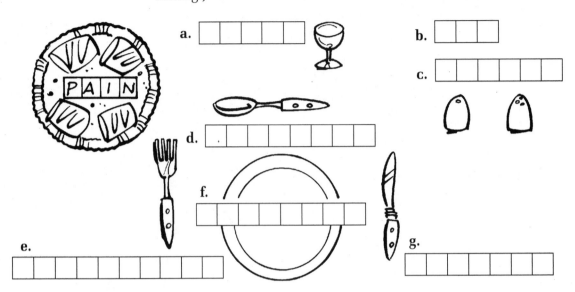

Exercise 3   Here is an extract from a letter. Can you write an English translation of it?

Les enfants grandissent. Moi, je grossis. Je voudrais maigrir, mais pour réussir à maigrir, il faut moins manger. Il faut choisir ... et moi, je finis par choisir la bonne cuisine française !

....

....

....

....

....

Exercise 4   First read through this conversation three times.

Anne   Pardon, Madame. Est-ce qu'il y a un restaurant par ici, s'il vous plaît?

Dame   Oui. Qu'est-ce que vous voulez comme restaurant?

Anne   Oh, un petit restaurant pas cher.

Dame   Alors, il y a un bistro à deux cents mètres sur la droite – ils ont une carte raisonnable, et un menu aussi, je crois. Ou bien vous avez un snack-bar dans la première rue à gauche, là – mais ils font uniquement des sandwichs, des hot dogs, des croque-monsieur, des choses comme ça.

Anne   Merci beaucoup, Madame.

Dame   Je vous en prie. Bon appétit!

Now write how you would tell someone in French:

There's a bar 100 meters on the left. They make sandwiches and pizzas. There is also a good little restaurant in the second street on the right. They have a reasonable set menu and you can eat à la carte too. Enjoy your meal!

....

....

....

....

....

....

Exercise 5   Various boat-operators in France offer cruises (**croisières**) lasting a few hours and including a large lunch or dinner. Here is the menu from one of them:

TARIFS et HORAIRES

Croisière gourmande
sur le bateau-restaurant
"Leconte de Lisle"

MENU Croisière comprise **300FF**

Servi au déjeuner et au dîner

MENU ENFANT (2 à 12 ans)

Croisière comprise **150FF**

Les repas sont entièrement réalisés à bord par notre chef

Terrine de Saint-Jacques
Saumon fumé
Médaillon de foie gras
Plateau de fruits de mer

Filet de truite de mer
Escalope de saumon
Caneton au poivre vert
Pièce de bœuf périgourdine

Fromage

Choix de dessert

You won't understand all the words in this menu. In real life, too, making intelligent guesses is a large part of getting along in a language. Make your best guesses in reply to these questions and then check your answers on page 60 before going on to exercise 6.

a.   Is the boat trip itself included in the price of the menu? ....

b.   Is this menu available in the evening? ....

c.   What is the French for 'smoked salmon'? ....

d.   What is the French for 'seafood'? ....

e.   What is the French for 'fillet of sea-trout'? ....

f.   What is the French for 'duckling with green pepper'?

....

g.   Which dishes should a non-meat-eater avoid?

....

h.   Are drinks included in the menu? ....

i.   Where and by whom are the meals cooked?

....

Exercise 6   Some (though not all) of these phrases belong in the blanks in the conversation below. Can you write in the correct ones?

> **Moi, je prends**   **quelques renseignements**
> **qu'est-ce que c'est que**   **qu'est-ce que vous avez comme**
> **Le service est compris?**   **la carte des vins**
> **c'est de la viande?**

Serveur	Messieurs-dames?
Client	Je voudrais .... , s'il vous plaît, Monsieur.
Serveur	Oui, bien sûr.
Client	La terrine de Saint-Jacques, ...
Serveur	Non, non, non. Les coquilles Saint-Jacques sont des fruits de mer.
Client	Ah, d'accord. Et .... la pièce de bœuf 'périgourdine'?
Serveur	Périgourdine, ça vient du Périgord – ça veut dire 'avec des truffes'.
Client	Ah, très bien. Alors, qu'est-ce que tu prends?
Cliente	Pour moi, la terrine de Saint-Jacques ...
Serveur	Oui ...
Cliente	... et l'escalope de saumon.
Serveur	Parfait. Et pour Monsieur?
	.... le plateau de fruits de mer et la pièce de bœuf périgourdine, s'il vous plaît.
Serveur	Très bien. Merci. Et qu'est-ce que vous désirez boire?
Client	Vous nous apportez .... , s'il vous plaît?
Serveur	Bien sûr, Monsieur.

ANSWERS

Exercise 1
une addition (bill), un verre (glass), une cuillère (spoon), des gens (people)

Exercise 2
a. verre **b.** sel **c.** poivre **d.** cuillère (also spelled **cuiller**)
e. fourchette **f.** assiette **g.** couteau

Exercise 3
... The children are growing taller. I'm growing fat. I'd like to lose weight, but to succeed in losing weight, you have to eat less. You have to choose ... and I always end up choosing good French food/cooking! (Remember that your answer does not have to be word-for-word the same.)

Exercise 4
Il y a un bar à cent mètres sur la gauche. Ils font des sandwichs et des pizzas. Il y a aussi un bon petit restaurant dans la deuxième rue à droite. Ils ont un menu raisonnable et on peut manger à la carte aussi. Bon appétit!
(Again, this is not the only possible correct translation. For example, you could equally well have put **à gauche** instead of **sur la gauche**, or **également** instead of **aussi**.)

Exercise 5
a. Yes (**croisière comprise** means 'cruise included') **b.** Yes (it is **servi au déjeuner et au dîner**, served at lunch and dinner)
c. Saumon fumé **d.** Fruits de mer **e.** Filet de truite de mer
f. Caneton au poivre vert **g.** Médaillon de foie gras, caneton au poivre vert, pièce de bœuf périgourdine (piece of beef cooked Périgord style – i.e. with truffles) **h.** No **i.** On board (**à bord**) by the boat's chef (**par notre chef**)

Exercise 6
Je voudrais quelques renseignements, s'il vous plaît, Monsieur. / La terrine de Saint-Jacques, c'est de la viande? / Ah, d'accord. Et qu'est-ce que c'est que la pièce de bœuf 'périgourdine'? / Moi, je prends le plateau de fruits de mer et la pièce de bœuf périgourdine, s'il vous plaît. / Vous nous apportez la carte des vins, s'il vous plaît?

Exercise 1 Your daughter's French penpal has written to her, describing the place where she lives. Read the extract from the letter three times before you try to answer the questions.

> Dans ce village il y a une boulangerie, un magasin d'alimentation et une boucherie. Il y a une très belle église du treizième siècle et les vestiges d'un château du quatorzième. Nous avons aussi un café dans le village, à deux cents mètres de notre maison — j'y vais souvent le samedi soir pour voir les amis. Sinon, pour aller au cinéma, pour danser, pour faire du sport, il faut aller en ville — normalement, nous prenons le bus pour y aller et puis Maman ou Papa vient nous chercher en voiture.

a. What stores are there in the village?

....

b. From which century does the church date?

....

c. And the remains of the château?

....

d. How far from the French girl's house is the village café?

....

e. When does she usually go there?

....

f. Where is the movie theater?

....

g. How does she usually get there?

....

h. How does she usually get back?

....

Exercise 2 The French girl's letter goes on to describe her likes and dislikes with regard to food:

> Pour la nourriture, je ne suis pas difficile :
> j'adore toutes les viandes, les salades, le fromage,
> les fruits... mais je déteste le mélange salé - sucré
> (jambon - ananas, par exemple). Je n'aime pas
> du tout le vin ou la bière et je n'aime pas
> beaucoup le thé.

a. What four things does the French girl say she likes?

....

b. What four things does she say she dislikes?

....

Exercise 3 Now you write back to the French girl's parents and explain your daughter's likes and dislikes. See if you can translate this into French.

> As far as food is concerned, my
> daughter is not difficult: she likes
> a lot of things, but she doesn't
> like tripe, she hates oysters and she
> can't stand snails.

Pour la nourriture, ...

....

....

....

....

....

Exercise 4   If you can't stand snails, you should say so! For this exercise, use your dictionary to look up one or more items of food or drink to which you personally react in each of the following ways, and then write out the sentence in French.

a.   I absolutely love (adore) ....

b.   I really like ....

c.   I like ....

d.   I don't really like ....

e.   I don't like ....

f.   I don't at all like ....

g.   I hate ....

h.   I can't stand ....

Obviously, the answers at the end of the unit can only give the verbs, but do take the time to write the other words – it will help you memorize them so that, in real life, you can avoid being presented with snails, tripe, horsemeat or whatever else your pet peeves are!

Exercise 5   Your chance to play matchmaker! Applicants to a dating service have written descriptions of their likes and dislikes. Here are some extracts. From the limited information available, can you pair up the men in the left-hand column with the women in the right-hand column who seem to have the most in common with them?

Hommes	Femmes
a. J'adore le sport. J'aime beaucoup regarder le football à la télévision et je joue au rugby le samedi. Je déteste les snobs et les intellectuels.	**1** J'aime la culture: le théâtre, le ballet, les concerts, le cinéma, les expositions. Pour la nourriture, j'aime beaucoup toutes les viandes, les poissons, les fruits de mer.
b. J'aime beaucoup aller au théâtre, aux concerts, aux musées. J'aime bien manger au restaurant. Pour la nourriture, je ne suis pas difficile: j'adore un bon steak-frites. J'aime aussi les spaghettis à la bolognaise, la cuisine chinoise, le couscous ... pratiquement tout, quoi!	**2** Je joue au tennis le samedi et je vais à la piscine le jeudi. Je suis très sportive. Par contre, je n'aime pas tout ce qu'on appelle 'culture': le théâtre, l'opéra, etc.
c. J'aime passionnément les langues: je parle français (bien sûr), anglais, allemand, espagnol et russe et j'apprends maintenant le japonais. Je n'ai pas beaucoup de temps libre pour aller au restaurant!	**3** J'aime beaucoup les animaux; j'ai horreur de manger de la viande et je n'aime pas beaucoup manger du poisson. Pour sortir, j'aime aller voir un bon film ou bien aller en discothèque.
d. Je ne sors pas souvent le soir, mais j'aime bien aller danser ou bien aller au cinéma. J'aime aussi aller manger dans un restaurant végétarien.	**4** Je vais à un cours du soir pour apprendre le chinois. Je parle déjà trois langues européennes. Le chinois est beaucoup plus difficile, mais c'est une langue fascinante. Je ne vais pas souvent au restaurant; si j'y vais, je mange surtout de la cuisine chinoise!

Exercise 6   Now look at what those same applicants say about where they choose to live. Some of the couples you put together in the last exercise no longer seem so compatible. Which of the pairs still have potential?

Hommes	Femmes
a. J'aime habiter dans une grande ville qui offre des possibilités sportives.	**1** Je déteste habiter en province. Pour moi, il faut absolument habiter en plein cœur de Paris.
b. Moi, je suis parisien et j'adore Paris. Pour moi, habiter en province, ce n'est vraiment pas intéressant, parce que c'est à Paris qu'on trouve les théâtres, l'opéra, les concerts, les musées.	**2** Je déteste la ville: avec le bruit et la pollution, la vie devient impossible en ville. J'aime habiter à la campagne où le rythme de la vie reste humain.
c. Je préfère habiter dans une petite ville de province. Je n'aime pas les grandes villes anonymes, mais je n'aime pas non plus habiter dans un petit village où il n'y a pas de cours du soir, pas de chemin de fer, pas de bus après sept heures du soir.	**3** Pour moi, l'idéal c'est d'habiter en plein centre d'une grande ville.
d. J'habite une vieille ferme à la campagne. C'est à côté d'un petit village de 200 habitants où je connais tout le monde. J'adore ça!	**4** Paris et les grandes villes, non merci. La vie en pleine campagne ne m'intéresse pas non plus. Je préfère vivre dans une petite ville où on peut connaître les gens, mais où il y a quand même des possibilités culturelles.

ANSWERS

Exercise 1

a. a baker's, a grocery store and a butcher's **b.** thirteenth **c.** fourteenth
d. 200 meters **e.** on Saturday evenings **f.** in town **g.** by bus **h.** her
mother or her father picks her up in the car.

Exercise 2

a. all kinds of meat, salads, cheese and fruit **b.** the mixture of
salty and sweet, wine, beer and tea

Exercise 3

Pour la nourriture, ma fille n'est pas difficile: elle aime beaucoup de
choses, mais elle n'aime pas la triperie, elle déteste les huîtres et elle
a horreur des escargots.

Exercise 4

a. J'adore ... **b.** J'aime beaucoup ... **c.** J'aime (bien) ... **d.** Je n'aime
pas beaucoup ... **e.** Je n'aime pas ... **f.** Je n'aime pas du tout ...
g. Je déteste ... **h.** J'ai horreur de ...

Exercise 5

a. 2 **b.** 1 **c.** 4 **d.** 3

Exercise 6

Only **b**/1 and **c**/4 still have potential: **a** and 2 no longer seem
compatible because he likes living in town and she hates it; **d** and 3
also have opposite preferences: he lives in an old farm near a
village with only 200 inhabitants and she likes living in the
center of a large town.

Exercise 1   Here is the **légende** (key) from a tourist map.

	ZONE VERTE		PHARE	C	ÉCOLE DE CANOË-KAYAK
	ZONE URBAINE		PROMENADE FLUVIALE ET MARITIME	I	POINTS D'INFORMATION
	PLAGE		SITE MÉGALITHIQUE		MOULIN
	PORT DE PECHE		CENTRE ÉQUESTRE		CHATEAU
	PORT DE PLAISANCE	V	ÉCOLE DE VOILE		CHAPELLE
	TENNIS	P	ÉCOLE DE PECHE		ÉGLISE

What is the French for each of the following?

a. urban area ....

b. megalithic site ....

c. fishing port ....

d. riding center ....

e. lighthouse ....

f. beach ....

g. sailing school ....

h. (wind)mill ....

i. pleasure port ....

Exercise 2   What about these other places? Can you remember how to write them in French?

a. a cathedral ....

b. a museum ....

c. a swimming pool ....

d. the sea ....

e. a bank ....

f. a bus station ....

Exercise 3   Here is a guidebook entry for Alençon in Normandy. Read it through three times and see how much of it you can understand, even though you don't know all the words. (One that you will need is **la dentelle**, 'lace.') When you have done that, try to answer the questions in French – you don't need to write full sentences.

ALENÇON

Département de l'Orne
32 526 habitants (les Alençonnais)
Paris 191 km, Le Mans 49 km

Située sur les bords de la Sarthe, la ville d'Alençon est encore aujourd'hui le principal marché d'une fertile campagne.

Principales curiosités

Église Notre-Dame – *visite ¼ heure* – Ce beau monument de style flamboyant date des 14e et 15e siècles.

Musée de Peinture – *dans l'hôtel de ville* – Des peintures des 17e, 18e et 19e siècles, parfaitement présentées.

Ancien château – Bâti au 14e et 15e siècles par Jean le Beau, premier duc d'Alençon. La forteresse, très restaurée, est maintenant transformée en prison.

Musée de la Dentelle – Une manufacture de dentelle fut créée à Alençon en 1665. De nos jours, une école dentellière maintient les traditions de cette belle industrie.

Maison d'Ozé – Cette jolie maison du 15e siècle abrite un musée d'histoire locale. Une collection d'antiquités gallo-romaines y est également présentée.

Chapelle Sainte-Thérèse – La chapelle est à côté de la maison natale de Sainte Thérèse de Lisieux (née le 2 janvier 1873).

---

a. Quel est le nom donné aux habitants d'Alençon?

....

b. Selon le guide, combien de temps faut-il pour visiter l'Église

Notre-Dame? ....

c. De quels siècles datent les peintures exposées dans l'hôtel

de ville? ....

d. Quel est maintenant le rôle de l'ancien château?

....

e. Depuis quand est-ce qu'on fabrique de la dentelle à Alençon?

....

f. Où est-ce que la Chapelle Sainte-Thérèse est située?

....

Exercise 4   **Quel temps fait-il?** There are often a number of ways of saying the same thing. As a quick review exercise, write '**S**' for 'Sunshine' or '**R**' for 'Rain' next to each of these statements:

a. Il fait beau. ....

b. Le soleil brille. ....

c. Il pleut. ....

d. Il fait un temps pluvieux. ....

e. Le temps est ensoleillé. ....

f. Il y a de la pluie. ....

g. Il y a des averses. ....

Exercise 5 You are the co-organizer of a conference to be held in Stratford, England—the town where William Shakespeare was born. Your French counterpart asks you to write an outline in French of the main attractions of the town. Can you do it? Here is the English version. Some of the phrases from exercise 3 will come in handy for translating it.

STRATFORD-UPON-AVON
Main places of interest

The birthplace of Shakespeare.

....

Hall's Croft, in the Old Town – the house of John Hall, the husband of Shakespeare's daughter.

....

....

The house of Anne Hathaway, Shakespeare's wife, at Shottery.

....

The house of Mary Arden, Shakespeare's mother, at Wilmcote.

....

Three theaters.

....

The town hall, built in the 18th century by Robert Newman.

....

A lot of houses which date from the 15th and 16th centuries.

....

A medieval chapel.

....

An interesting market.

....

Exercise 6 Can you match up these half-sentences to reflect the weather conditions shown on the map?

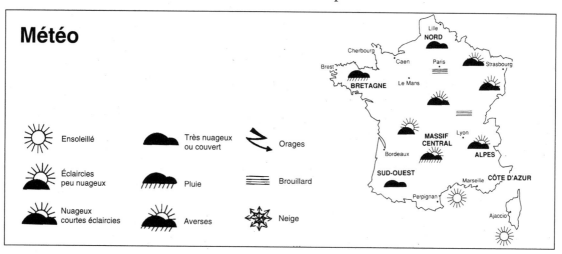

Météo

Ensoleillé	Très nuageux ou couvert	Orages
Éclaircies peu nuageux	Pluie	Brouillard
Nuageux courtes éclaircies	Averses	Neige

a. **En Bretagne**	1 **il y a du brouillard.**
b. **Sur la Côte d'Azur**	2 **le soleil brille.**
c. **Dans le Massif Central**	3 **il pleut.**
d. **Dans les Alpes**	4 **il y a des averses.**
e. **Dans la région parisienne**	5 **il y a des nuages.**
f. **Dans le Nord de la France**	6 **il fait un temps nuageux avec de courtes éclaircies.**

Exercise 7 Fill in the French words for:

1 Snow (5)
2 Sunny intervals (10)
3 Cold (5)
4 Sunny (10)
5 Cloudy (7)

6 Hot (5)
7 Fine (4)
8 Fog (10)
9 Winds (5)

ANSWERS

Exercise 1

a. zone urbaine **b.** site mégalithique **c.** port de pêche **d.** centre équestre **e.** phare **f.** plage **g.** école de voile **h.** moulin **i.** port de plaisance

Exercise 2

a. une cathédrale **b.** un musée **c.** une piscine **d.** la mer **e.** une banque **f.** une gare routière

Exercise 3

a. les Alençonnais **b.** un quart d'heure **c.** des 17e, 18e et 19e siècles **d.** c'est une prison **e.** depuis 1665 **f.** à côté de la maison natale de la sainte

Exercise 4

a. S **b.** S **c.** R **d.** R **e.** S **f.** R **g.** R

Exercise 5

This was a difficult exercise and it would be very surprising if you managed to do it without making any mistakes. Remember too that the translation which follows is only one possible version:

STRATFORD-UPON-AVON
Principales curiosités:
La maison natale de Shakespeare.
Hall's Croft, dans la Vieille Ville – la maison de John Hall, le mari de la fille de Shakespeare.
La maison d'Anne Hathaway, la femme de Shakespeare, à Shottery.
La maison de Mary Arden, la mère de Shakespeare, à Wilmcote.
Trois théâtres.
L'hôtel de ville, bâti au 18e siècle par Robert Newman.
Beaucoup de maisons qui datent des 15e et 16e siècles.
Une chapelle moyenâgeuse.
Un marché intéressant.

Exercise 6

a. 3 **b.** 2 **c.** 4 **d.** 6 **e.** 1 **f.** 5

Exercise 7

Exercise 1 The names of 14 countries appear in this word square, written either across (left-to-right) or down. Can you write out the names of these countries? When you do so, it would be a good idea to look up their genders and write **le**, **la**, **l'** or **les**, as appropriate, with each name.

M	I	A	E	L	B	T	A	C	I	L	A
E	T	G	C	E	E	A	J	A	N	P	U
C	A	R	H	O	L	L	A	N	D	E	T
O	L	E	I	P	G	G	P	A	E	S	R
S	I	C	N	H	I	H	O	D	O	P	I
S	E	E	E	I	Q	U	N	A	V	A	C
E	T	A	T	S	U	N	I	S	E	G	H
S	U	I	S	S	E	E	R	T	U	N	E
P	A	Y	S	D	E	G	A	L	L	E	S

....

....

....

....

....

....

....

....

....

....

....

....

....

Exercise 2   Here are some ads for French gîtes:

> **Gîtes de France**

---

1 **Pour 6/7 personnes**: pavillon récemment rénové, situé à un kilomètre du village d'Ozeille (magasin d'alimentation, boulangerie, café, église).
Au rez-de-chaussée: salon-salle à manger, cuisine, salle de bains.
Au premier étage (accès difficile pour personnes infirmes): une chambre avec un grand lit, une chambre à deux lits, une chambre avec un grand lit et un lit individuel.
Au deuxième étage: grenier vide – idéal pour les enfants quand il pleut!

2 **Pour 6/7 personnes**: maison confortable à côté d'une ferme à cinq kilomètres du village de Cressy (hôtel, restaurant, magasins, église).
Au rez-de-chaussée: salon-salle-à-manger-cuisine, une chambre pour une personne, toilettes, salle d'eau.
Au premier étage: deux chambres doubles, une chambre à deux lits, salle de bains.

3 **Pour 6/7 personnes**: appartement au premier étage d'une belle maison du 17e siècle en plein centre d'Angers.
Salon, salle-à-manger-cuisine, salle de bains, toilettes séparées, trois chambres: deux chambres à deux lits et une chambre avec un grand lit et un lit individuel.

---

a. If you were going on vacation with someone who could not climb stairs, which of these gîtes would you choose? ....

b. If six friends wanted a vacation home where they did not have to share beds, which of these places would suit them? ....

c. Which would be the one to choose if you wanted to be in a town instead of in the country? ....

d. Which one is proposed as being particularly good for children (provided they are big enough to use difficult stairs)?

....

Exercise 3   Here is the life story of a language junkie. Try reading it through three times. You won't know all the words, but see if you can understand enough to answer the questions below.

> Ma langue maternelle est l'anglais. J'ai commencé le français à l'âge de onze ans à l'école. A partir de l'âge de douze ans, j'ai fait du latin, et puis à seize ans j'ai commencé à apprendre le grec ancien. A vingt et un ans, j'ai suivi un cours de grec moderne. Ensuite, j'ai vécu en France pendant un an; j'ai donc beaucoup parlé français pendant cette période. Dix ans plus tard, j'ai de nouveau habité sur le territoire français, mais cette fois à l'île de la Réunion, dans l'Océan Indien. Là, j'ai appris un peu de créole réunionnais – c'est une langue basée sur le français. A trente-trois ans j'ai appris l'allemand pour mon travail, puis à trente-cinq ans j'ai étudié l'italien pour mon plaisir. J'ai fait un tout petit peu de japonais, en allant à un cours du soir pendant trois mois, mais c'est une langue vraiment difficile. Maintenant j'apprends le russe: je vais à un cours du soir et je travaille à la maison avec un livre et des cassettes. Il faut dire que j'aime beaucoup les langues!

a.   What is the writer's mother tongue? ....

b.   At what age did she start French? ....

c.   What was the next language she learned? ....

d.   At what age did she start Ancient Greek? ....

e.   Where is the island of Reunion? ....

f.   On which language is Reunionese Creole based? ....

g.   Why did the writer learn German? ....

h.   Which language does she say she learned just for pleasure?

....

i.   Which language did she find particularly difficult?

....

j.   How is she studying Russian?

....

....

Exercise 4   Be positive! Answer these questions with **Oui** and a full sentence.

Example   **Oui, j'ai étudié le français à l'école.**

a.   **Avez-vous étudié le français à l'école?**

....

b.   **Avez-vous appris d'autres langues?**

....

c.   **Avez-vous parlé français avec des Français?**

....

d.   **Est-ce que vous avez beaucoup voyagé en France?**

....

e.   **Est-ce que vous avez vu le château de Versailles?**

....

f.   **Est-ce que vous avez visité les Pyrénées?**

....

g.   **Avez-vous compris les menus dans les restaurants français?**

....

Now, in a negative frame of mind, see if you can answer each of those same questions with **Non** and a full sentence.

Example   **Non, je n'ai pas étudié le français à l'école.**

h.   ....

i.   ....

j.   ....

k.   ....

l.   ....

m.   ....

n.   ....

Exercise 5   The words missing from the letter opposite are past participles from the verbs in the box. Can you write the correct forms in the blanks? Each verb is used once only.

New word: **louer** (to rent)

manger	apprendre	voyager	boire	louer	prendre
quitter	oublier	visiter	passer	lire	dormir

Nous avons passé de très bonnes vacances cette année: nous avons .... en Écosse. Nous avons donc .... Reims à six heures du matin. Nous avons .... l'avion au départ de Paris-Charles de Gaulle – un vol sur Édimbourg. Nous avons .... la nuit en ville et puis nous avons .... une voiture pour aller à notre gîte. Là, nous avons .... les problèmes du travail; nous avons bien .... ; nous avons .... du haggis; nous avons .... du whisky; nous avons .... le journal local et nous avons .... quelques monuments de la région. Nous avons même .... à parler anglais avec un accent écossais!

Exercise 6   You are staying with French friends. You have lost your watch somewhere in their apartment. You tell your friends and they ask which rooms you have been in this morning. Write in the spaces how you will tell them in French what your movements have been. You will need the words **la montre** (watch), **bien sûr** (of course), **laisser** (to leave).

a.   I have lost my watch.

....

b.   I slept in my bedroom, of course.

....

c.   I took a shower in the bathroom.

....

d.   I made some coffee in the kitchen.

....

e.   I drank my coffee and I read the newspaper in the dining room.

....

f.   I watched television in the living room.

....

g.   I worked in the study.

....

h.   Ah! I know! I left my watch in the study!

ANSWERS

Exercise 1

Across: la Hollande, les États-Unis (masc. plural), la Suisse, le Pays de Galles

Down: l'Écosse (fem.), l'Italie (fem.), la Grèce, la Chine, la Belgique, le Japon, le Canada, l'Inde (fem.), l'Espagne (fem.), l'Autriche (fem.)

Exercise 2

a. 2 **b.** 3 **c.** 3 **d.** 1

Exercise 3

a. English **b.** eleven **c.** Latin **d.** sixteen **e.** in the Indian Ocean
f. French **g.** for her work **h.** Italian **i.** Japanese **j.** She goes to an evening class and she works at home with a book and cassettes.

Exercise 4

a. Oui, j'ai étudié le français à l'école. **b.** Oui, j'ai appris d'autres langues. **c.** Oui, j'ai parlé français avec des Français. **d.** Oui, j'ai beaucoup voyagé en France. **e.** Oui, j'ai vu le château de Versailles.
f. Oui, j'ai visité les Pyrénées. **g.** Oui, j'ai compris les menus dans les restaurants français. **h.** Non, je n'ai pas étudié le français à l'école.
i. Non, je n'ai pas appris d'autres langues. **j.** Non, je n'ai pas parlé français avec des Français. **k.** Non, je n'ai pas beaucoup voyagé en France. **l.** Non, je n'ai pas vu le château de Versailles. **m.** Non, je n'ai pas visité les Pyrénées. **n.** Non, je n'ai pas compris les menus dans les restaurants français.

Exercise 5

Nous avons passé de très bonnes vacances cette année: nous avons **voyagé** en Écosse. Nous avons donc **quitté** Reims à six heures du matin. Nous avons **pris** l'avion au départ de Paris-Charles de Gaulle – un vol sur Édimbourg. Nous avons **passé** la nuit en ville et puis nous avons **loué** une voiture pour aller à notre gîte. Là, nous avons **oublié** les problèmes du travail; nous avons bien **dormi**; nous avons **mangé** du haggis; nous avons **bu** du whisky; nous avons **lu** le journal local et nous avons **visité** quelques monuments de la région. Nous avons même **appris** à parler anglais avec un accent écossais!

Exercise 6

a. J'ai perdu ma montre. **b.** J'ai dormi dans ma chambre, bien sûr.
c. J'ai pris une douche dans la salle de bains. **d.** J'ai fait du café dans la cuisine. **e.** J'ai bu mon café et j'ai lu le journal dans la salle à manger. **f.** J'ai regardé la télévision dans le salon / dans la salle de séjour. **g.** J'ai travaillé dans le bureau. **h.** Ah! Je sais! J'ai laissé ma montre dans le bureau!

14 STATING YOUR INTENTIONS

Exercise 1   Here are some basic sentence patterns:

Past   **J'ai   fini mon travail.**
I have   finished my work.
This also translates 'I finished my work.'

Future   **Je vais   finir mon travail.**
I am going   to finish my work.

Note also   **J'espère   finir mon travail.**
I hope   to finish my work.

In **a–k** below, only one of the options on the right (**1** or **2**) is a possible completion for each of the sentences begun on the left. Can you check the correct box in each case?

a.   **J'espère**   ☐ 1   **voyagé en Chine.**
                    ☐ 2   **voyager en Chine.**

b.   **Je vais**   ☐ 1   **vu la Tour Eiffel.**
                    ☐ 2   **voir la Tour Eiffel.**

c.   **J'ai**   ☐ 1   **visité le Musée du Louvre.**
                    ☐ 2   **visiter le Musée du Louvre.**

d.   **J'ai**   ☐ 1   **beaucoup travaillé.**
                    ☐ 2   **beaucoup travailler.**

e.   **Tu vas**   ☐ 1   **pris le métro.**
                    ☐ 2   **prendre le métro.**

f.   **Ils espèrent**   ☐ 1   **eu des enfants.**
                        ☐ 2   **avoir des enfants.**

g.   **Tu as**   ☐ 1   **compris?**
                    ☐ 2   **comprendre?**

h.   **Il a**   ☐ 1   **écrit une lettre.**
                    ☐ 2   **écrire une lettre.**

i.   **Nous avons**   ☐ 1   **dormi.**
                      ☐ 2   **dormir.**

j.   **Nous allons**   ☐ 1   **appris l'italien.**
                       ☐ 2   **apprendre l'italien.**

k.   **Elle va**   ☐ 1   **été contente.**
                    ☐ 2   **être contente.**

Exercise 2   A fortune teller spins this tale to an impressionable client:

Vous allez beaucoup voyager. Vous allez partir au Canada et vous allez travailler dans un bureau. Là, vous allez vous marier avec votre patron. Vous et votre mari, vous allez devenir riches et vous allez avoir un bel appartement en ville et une très grande maison au bord de la mer. Vous et votre mari, vous allez avoir trois enfants: un garçon et deux filles. Votre mari va mourir à 93 ans; vous, vous allez vivre jusqu'à l'âge de 95 ans.

The client writes to a friend, relaying the predictions. Can you complete this paragraph of her letter?

Je vais beaucoup voyager. Je ....

....

....

....

....

....

....

....

....

jusqu'à l'âge de 95 ans.

Exercise 3 Remembering that you use **avoir** to express age (e.g., **J'ai 22 ans**, 'I am 22'), how would you say each of the following?

   a. How old are you? (to a child)

....

   b. How old are you? (to someone you call **vous**)

....

   c. I am going to be forty-two on July 14.

....

   d. Jean is going to be thirty-nine on December 23.

....

   e. Michel is going to be sixty on March 27.

....

   f. You are going to be three years old tomorrow!

....

Exercise 4 How will these children say they are going to do what their heroes do?

   Example **Maman est pilote.**
   Moi aussi, je vais être pilote.

   a. **Ma sœur est comptable.**

   Moi aussi, ...

   b. **Papa joue au golf.**

   Moi aussi, ...

   c. **Mon frère va à l'université.**

   Moi aussi, ...

   d. **Maman travaille à Versailles.**

   Moi aussi, ...

   e. **Jean-Claude fait des reportages dans les pays étrangers.**

   Moi aussi, ...

   f. **Isabelle fait un stage dans une école à Paris.**

   Moi aussi, ...

Exercise 5   Meet Frédéric, who is about to put some clothes on!

Can you remember the names and genders of the clothes illustrated? Try to write out a sentence about each one, following the pattern in the example.

Example   **Il va mettre son pull.** (He's going to put his sweater on.)

Be careful to use the right form of **son**, **sa** and **ses**.

a.   ....

b.   ....

c.   ....

d.   ....

e.   ....

f.   ....

g.   ....

Exercise 6   Here is part of a letter from a French friend, telling you about his family's upcoming vacation. You can probably guess that **pique-niquer** means 'to picnic.'

Nous allons, bien sûr, visiter les monuments intéressants de la région : il y a une cathédrale du treizième siècle et trois châteaux à voir. Notre hôtel est à 500 mètres de la plage, alors nous allons faire de la natation. S'il fait beau, les enfants vont jouer au football; s'il pleut, ils vont jouer au ping-pong! Ils vont aussi faire du cheval : il y a une école d'équitation tout près. Moi, je vais lire quatre ou cinq livres : c'est un élément essentiel des vacances pour moi. A midi, nous allons proballement pique-niquer et puis, le soir, nous allons dîner au restaurant.

Use the language of that letter to help you write to another friend about your own vacation plans:

During our vacation, we are going to visit the châteaux of the Loire. The children are also going to ride. Lee is going to read and **I** am going to do some swimming. Our hotel is in Tours and there is a swimming pool nearby. At noon, we will eat a pizza or a hot dog and then, in the evening, we will have dinner at the hotel.

....

....

....

....

....

....

....

ANSWERS

Exercise 1
a. 2 **b.** 2 **c.** 1 **d.** 1 **e.** 2 **f.** 2 **g.** 1 **h.** 1 **i.** 1 **j.** 2 **k.** 2

Exercise 2
Je vais beaucoup voyager. Je vais partir au Canada et je vais travailler dans un bureau. Là, je vais me marier avec mon patron. Mon mari et moi, nous allons devenir riches et nous allons avoir un bel appartement en ville et une très grande maison au bord de la mer. Mon mari et moi, nous allons avoir trois enfants: un garçon et deux filles. Mon mari va mourir à 93 ans; moi, je vais vivre jusqu'à l'âge de 95 ans.

Exercise 3
a. Quel âge as-tu? (OR Tu as quel âge?) **b.** Quel âge avez-vous? (OR Vous avez quel âge?) **c.** Je vais avoir quarante-deux ans le 14 juillet. **d.** Jean va avoir trente-neuf ans le 23 décembre. **e.** Michel va avoir soixante ans le 27 mars. **f.** Tu vas avoir trois ans demain!

Exercise 4
a. je vais être comptable **b.** je vais jouer au golf **c.** je vais aller à l'université **d.** je vais travailler à Versailles **e.** je vais faire des reportages dans les pays étrangers **f.** je vais faire un stage dans une école à Paris

Exercise 5
a. Il va mettre son slip. **b.** Il va mettre son pantalon. **c.** Il va mettre ses chaussettes. **d.** Il va mettre ses chaussures. **e.** Il va mettre sa chemise. **f.** Il va mettre sa veste. **g.** Il va mettre son manteau.

Exercise 6
Pendant les vacances, nous allons visiter les châteaux de la Loire. Les enfants vont aussi faire du cheval (OR faire de l'équitation). Lee va lire et moi, je vais faire de la natation. Notre hôtel est à Tours et il y a une piscine tout près. A midi, nous allons manger une pizza ou un hot dog, et puis, le soir, nous allons dîner à l'hôtel.

Exercise 1   Here is part of a letter from a French friend called Joëlle:

> Samedi matin, <u>je suis allée</u> faire des courses, puis,
> l'après-midi, je suis allée au Musée d'Orsay – c'était
> fabuleux! Le soir, Georges et moi, nous sommes sortis
> dîner chez des amis à Versailles. Nous sommes rentrés à
> la maison vers deux heures du matin. Dimanche, les
> parents de Georges sont venus 'déjeuner': ils sont
> arrivés à dix heures du matin et ils sont partis à dix
> heures du soir! C'est dimanche aussi que notre nièce
> Céline est née! Son père Alain a téléphoné à minuit pour
> nous annoncer la nouvelle!

First underline the verbs in the letter which are past tenses
using the verb **être** (**je suis**, **tu es**, **il est**, etc.). The first one has
been done for you. Then see if you can answer the following
questions in full French sentences, paying particular attention
to the forms of the verbs.

a.   **Qu'est-ce que Joëlle a fait samedi après-midi?**

....

b.   **Qu'est-ce que Joëlle et Georges ont fait samedi soir?**

....

c.   **A quelle heure est-ce qu'ils sont rentrés à la maison?**

....

d.   **A quelle heure est-ce que les parents de Georges sont arrivés
dimanche matin?**

....

e.   **A quelle heure est-ce qu'ils sont partis?**

....

f.   **Quelle est la grande nouvelle d'Alain?**

....

Exercise 2 As Exercise 1 reminded you, the main verbs of motion form their past tense with the verb **être** rather than **avoir**, e.g., **je suis allé** (written by a man), **je suis allée** (written by a woman). To refresh your memory on the past participles of these verbs, see if you can fill in the grid. (Although accents are not usually used in crosswords, it would be a good idea to write them in this case because accents distinguish between, for example, **je monte** and **je suis monté**.)

Example Clue: gone (f. pl.)   Answer: **allées**
Clue: gone (m. pl.)   Answer: **allés**

m. = masculine, f. = feminine, sing. = singular and pl. = plural.

1 died (m. pl.)
2 gone down (m. sing.)
3 stayed (m. sing.)
4 fallen (f. pl.)
5 arrived (f. sing.)
6 gone out (f. sing.)
7 left (m. sing.)
8 come (m. sing.)
9 gone up (m. sing.)
10 born (m. sing.)
11 entered (m. pl.)

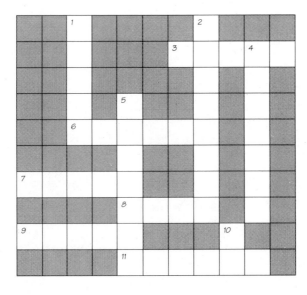

Exercise 3 The words in the box need to be written in the correct blanks in this recounting of the author's time on the French island of Reunion in the Indian Ocean.

New expression: **dans le vide** (into the void)

> ai   morte   suis   ingénieurs   descendue   est
> montagnes   tombée   rester   suis   partie   eu   est

A l'âge de trente-deux ans, je suis .... à la Réunion, dans l'Océan Indien. C'est une très belle île volcanique, avec de magnifiques .... et une végétation tropicale absolument fabuleuse. Je .... arrivée à la Réunion en septembre. En octobre, une vieille tante est .... en Angleterre; elle m'a très gentiment laissé £2000, alors j'...................... pu m'acheter une voiture. J'ai loué une maison dans un village à la montagne; en fait, le nom du village était La Montagne!

En janvier, nous avons .... très, très chaud et l'humidité était à 100%. C'était une 'dépression tropicale'. Puis, un soir, j'ai fini mon travail en ville et je .... montée chez moi au village comme d'habitude. Pendant la nuit, un vrai cyclone .... arrivé. J'ai donc dû .... à la maison pendant quatre jours de pluie torrentielle. Pendant le cyclone, la route de La Montagne est littéralement .... dans le vide, alors mon village .... resté pendant encore cinq jours complètement isolé de la ville. Pendant ce temps, les .... de l'île ont réussi à construire une sorte de pont pour permettre aux voitures de passer. Au bout de dix jours, je suis donc .... en ville et j'ai pu reprendre mon travail.

Exercise 4   Here is the program for a weekend in Paris. Imagine that you and your partner have been on the trip and are telling friends about it. Write out what you would say to them, giving the times and numbers in words rather than figures. To keep it from getting too complicated, leave out the words in parentheses, such as '(**dîner + visite de Paris la nuit**)'.

Tip   All the verbs you will need for this exercise take **être** in the past tense, so they will all begin with **nous sommes**.

You should start by saying: **Le vendredi, nous sommes partis de Lisieux à seize heures vingt et une.** You can take your choice for Sunday morning!

VENDREDI

16 h 21:
Départ de Lisieux

18 h 22:
Arrivée à Paris-St-Lazare

20 h 00:
Sortie (dîner + visite de
Paris la nuit)

1 h 00:
Retour à l'hôtel

SAMEDI

10 h 00:
On va dans les grands
magasins

14 h 00:
Descente dans les
catacombes

19 h 00:
Montée au 2e étage de la
Tour Eiffel
(dîner + panorama)

DIMANCHE

10 h 00:
On va à l'église – ou on
reste au lit!

12 h 00:
Montée au 56e étage de la
Tour Maine-Montparnasse
(déjeuner + panorama)

19 h 05:
Départ de Paris-St-Lazare

20 h 49: Arrivée à Lisieux

Exercise 5   Congratulations on working all the way through the book!
This last exercise is a quick review of the language covered
since Unit 1. It is based on the old game where you have to try
not to say 'Yes' or 'No'. Do it aloud the first time through,
finding ways of answering which do not include **Oui** or **Non**,
and then write out your answers.

Example   For **a** you might put **Je suis en vacances** OR **Je ne suis pas en
vacances.**

a.   **Vous êtes en vacances?**

....

b.   **Vous êtes célibataire?**

....

c.   **Qu'est-ce que vous prenez pour le petit déjeuner?**

....

d.   **Où peut-on changer des chèques de voyage dans votre ville?**

....

e.   **Pour aller à la gare, s'il vous plaît?**

....

f.   **A quelle heure est-ce que vous vous levez normalement?**

....

g.   **Où peut-on acheter du pain dans votre ville?**

....

h.   **Avez-vous mal à la tête?**

....

i.   **Est-ce que le train est moins cher que l'avion aux Etats-Unis?**

....

j.   **Est-ce que le service est compris normalement dans les
restaurants américains?**

....

k.   **Aimez-vous la cuisine française?**

....

l.   **Est-ce que la mer est proche de chez vous?**

....

m.   **Parlez-vous allemand?**

....

n.   **Qu'est-ce que vous allez faire demain?**

....

o.   **Etes-vous allé(e) en France?**

....

ANSWERS

Exercise 1

You should have underlined: (je suis allée), je suis allée, nous sommes sortis, nous sommes rentrés, (les parents de Georges) sont venus, ils sont arrivés, ils sont partis, (notre nièce Céline) est née **a.** Elle est allée au Musée d'Orsay. **b.** Ils sont sortis dîner chez des amis à Versailles. **c.** Ils sont rentrés vers deux heures du matin. **d.** Ils sont arrivés à dix heures du matin. **e.** Ils sont partis à dix heures du soir. **f.** Sa fille Céline est née dimanche.

Exercise 2

Exercise 3

partie; montagnes; suis; morte; ai; eu; suis; est; rester; tombée; est; ingénieurs; descendue

Exercise 4

Le vendredi, nous sommes partis de Lisieux à seize heures vingt et une. Nous sommes arrivés à Paris-St-Lazare à dix-huit heures vingt-deux. Nous sommes sortis à vingt heures et nous sommes retournés à l'hôtel à une heure du matin.

Le samedi, nous sommes allés dans les grands magasins à dix heures. Nous sommes descendus dans les catacombes à quatorze heures. Nous sommes montés au deuxième étage de la Tour Eiffel à dix-neuf heures.

Le dimanche matin, nous sommes allés à l'église à dix heures (OR nous sommes restés au lit). Nous sommes montés au cinquante-sixième étage de la Tour Maine-Montparnasse à midi. Nous sommes partis de Paris-St-Lazare à dix-neuf heures cinq et nous sommes arrivés à Lisieux à vingt heures quarante-neuf.

Exercise 5

There can be, of course, many answers to this exercise, but here is one possible set: **a.** Je ne suis pas en vacances. **b.** Je suis marié(e).**c.** Pour le petit déjeuner, je prends du café au lait, du pain et du beurre. **d.** On peut changer des chèques de voyage à la banque. **e.** Vous allez tout droit, vous prenez la troisième rue à gauche et puis la première à droite. **f.** Je me lève à huit heures normalement. **g.** A la boulangerie ou au supermarché. **h.** Je n'ai pas mal à la tête. **i.** Il est vrai que le train est normalement moins cher que l'avion aux Etats-Unis. **j.** En général, le service n'est pas compris dans les restaurants américains. **k.** J'adore la cuisine française! **l.** La mer n'est pas proche de chez nous. **m.** Je ne parle pas allemand. **n.** Demain je vais travailler et puis, le soir, je vais aller au cinéma. **o.** Bien sûr!

FOREIGN LANGUAGE BOOKS

Multilingual
The Insult Dictionary: How to Give 'Em Hell in 5 Nasty Languages
The Lover's Dictionary: How to be Amorous in 5 Delectable Languages
Handbook for Multilingual Business Writing
Multilingual Phrase Book
Let's Drive Europe Phrasebook
Talk Your Way Around Europe Phrasebook
Thomas Cook European Rail Traveler's Phrasebook
CD-ROM "Languages of the World": Multilingual Dictionary Database

Spanish
NTC's Beginner's Spanish and English Dictionary
Vox Spanish and English Dictionaries
Cervantes-Walls Spanish and English Dictionary
NTC's Dictionary of Spanish False Cognates
Nice 'n Easy Spanish Grammar
Spanish Verbs and Essentials of Grammar
Spanish Grammar in Review
Getting Started in Spanish
Spanish Culture Coloring Book
El Alfabeto
Spanish à la Cartoon
101 Spanish Idioms
Guide to Spanish Idioms
Guide to Spanish Suffixes
Guide to Correspondence in Spanish
The Hispanic Way
Al Corriente: Expressions Needed for Communicating in Everyday Spanish

French
NTC's New College French and English Dictionary
French Verbs and Essentials of Grammar
Real French
Getting Started in French
Guide to French Idioms
Guide to Correspondence in French
French Culture Coloring Book
L'Alphabet
French à la Cartoon
101 French Idioms
Nice 'n Easy French Grammar
NTC's Beginner's French and English Dictionary
NTC's Dictionary of Faux Amis
NTC's Dictionary of Canadian French
NTC's French and English Business Dictionary
Au courant: Expressions for Communicating in Everyday French
The French Way

German
Schöffler-Weis German and English Dictionary
NTC's Beginner's German and English Dictionary
Klett German and English Dictionary
Klett Super-Mini German and English Dictionary
Guide to Correspondence in German
Getting Started in German
German Verbs and Essentials of Grammar
Guide to German Idioms
Streetwise German
Nice 'n Easy German Grammar
German à la Cartoon
NTC's Dictionary of German False Cognates

Italian
Zanichelli Super-Mini Italian and English Dictionary
Zanichelli New College Italian and English Dictionary
NTC's Beginner's Italian and English Dictionary
Getting Started in Italian
Italian Verbs and Essentials of Grammar
The Italian Way

Greek
NTC's New College Greek and English Dictionary

Latin
Essentials of Latin Grammar
Teach Yourself Latin

Hebrew
Everyday Hebrew

Chinese
Easy Chinese Phrasebook and Dictionary
Basic Chinese Vocabulary Dictionary

Korean
Korean in Plain English

Polish
The Wiedza Powszechna Compact Polish and English Dictionary

Swedish
Swedish Verbs and Essentials of Grammar

Russian
Easy Russian Phrasebook and Dictionary
Complete Handbook of Russian Verbs
NTC's Compact Russian and English Dictionary
Essentials of Russian Grammar
Business Russian
Roots of the Russian Language
Basic Structure Practice in Russian
The Russian Way

Japanese
Easy Japanese
Easy Kana Workbook
Easy Hiragana
Easy Katakana
101 Japanese Idioms
Konnichi wa Japan
NTC's Dictionary of Japan's Cultural Code Ways
Japanese in Plain English
Everyday Japanese
Japanese for Children
Japanese Cultural Encounters
Japanese for the Travel Industry
Nissan's Business Japanese

"Just Enough" Phrase Books
Chinese, Dutch, French, German, Greek, Hebrew, Hungarian, Italian, Japanese, Portuguese, Russian, Scandinavian, Serbo-Croat, Spanish
Business French, Business German, Business Spanish
BBC Phrase Books
French, Spanish, German, Italian, Greek, Arabic, Turkish, Portuguese

Audio and Video Language Programs
Just Listen 'n Learn Spanish, French, German, Italian, Japanese, Greek, and Arabic, Business Spanish, Business French, Business German, Arabi, Turkish
Just Listen 'n Learn...Spanish, French, German PLUS
Speak...Spanish, French, German, Japanese, Russian
Conversational...Spanish, French, German, Italian, Russian, Greek, Japanese, Thai, Portuguese in 7 Days
Practice & Improve Your...Spanish, French, Italian, and German
Practice & Improve Your...Spanish, French, Italian, and German PLUS
Improve Your...Spanish, French, Italian, and German: The P&I Method
VideoPassport French
VideoPassport Spanish
How to Pronounce...Spanish, French, German, Italian, Russian, Japanese Correctly
Verb Drill Series
French, Spanish, German, Italian
By Association Series
Spanish, French, German, Italian
How to Pronounce Series
Spanish, French

PASSPORT BOOKS
a division of *NTC Publishing Group*
Lincolnwood, Illinois USA